Solomon Returns Home

Solomon Returns Home

R Bhakther Solomon

Vitasta

Vitasta Publishing Pvt. Ltd.
New Delhi

Published by
Renu Kaul Verma for
Vitasta Publishing Pvt. Ltd.
2/15, Ansari Road, Daryaganj,
New Delhi - 110 002

ISBN 978-81-89766-56-6

Reprint 2010

Illustration by Abhimanyu Sinha
Typeset by Vitasta Publishing Pvt. Ltd.
Printed by Vits Press, New Delhi

Dedicated to my parents

Late Mr M Joseph Raj and Late Mrs Selviyal Sarojini

Contents

Acknowledgements

I gratefully acknowledge all those who have helped me in my first venture of authoring a book.

Foremost among them, I wish to thank God Almighty from the bottom of my heart for guiding me in my reminiscences as I faithfully recorded them in this book. I am overwhelmed with reverence and amazement at the way He has led me all the time in the vicissitudes of my life and has enabled me even amidst adverse circumstances to respond to His calling to the best of my ability.

I recall with gratitude how my parents, late Mr Joseph Raj and Mrs Selviyal Sarojini, helped me through their wisdom and care to rise from the ditch where I had once fallen and how they, with their unrelenting faith in God, enabled me to complete my collegiate education so that I could share the platform with church leaders and celebrities in ministering to the weaker sections of the society.

My heartfelt thanks to my wife Angeline Sulochana for all her selfless support and her patience despite my absence from home due to my work. She has been, is and always will be the most caring person taking all things in her stride quietly. She has been a pillar of support for me and has provided me with the strength required to reach out to others in need.

To my daughter Vanitha and my son Praveen Joseph, I owe my thanks. But for their encouragement, I would not have embarked on this mission of recollecting and narrating the story of my life.

I am also thankful to my secretary Mrs D Lalitha Kannan, who helped me in bringing out the first draft of the electronic copy of the manuscript.

Thanks is also due to Ms Soba Ramachandran for reading the first draft and giving her valuable inputs and advice.

I cannot afford to forget Renu Kaul Verma, my publisher, and Aastha Sharma for their hard work in making the book what it is.

R Bhakther Solomon

Preface

On my 60th birthday, it was my son Praveen Joseph who suggested that I should compile my life's experiences in a book for public reading. However, my wife Angeline Sulochana felt that no one, including herself, would read my stuff and that I should not waste my time in a futile exercise! For many months, I mulled over this and eventually decided that I should pen down something in writing so that at least my son would get to read it and be happy.

Writing an autobiography does provide a cathartic experience for the writer, enabling him to not just record the episodes of interest to the readers, but purging his own inner-self while recording those incidents that moulded the character of what he is today. My time spent away from home and the lessons life taught me then is the theme of the book. A runaway boy, rescued and restored to life's mainstream—that is my story.

The story of my own life scripted in the third person may read like fiction, but in reality it is not. It is the true story of a successful person who, from the pit of destruction, rose to a high position in the chosen field of service. No one could have imagined then that I would end up doing what I do now. It is a confirmation of the reality of the presence of God in human struggles as averred in *Isaiah 43:2.* The young boy in this book was guided by Almighty at a time when he was standing at crossroads, not knowing what to do next and wondering whether his Creator had forgotten him. This happens to almost everyone. In times of difficulties, it may seem that He has forsaken us. On the contrary, when one goes through hardships and sufferings, He reveals his amazing grace by recreating the person to make an impact in life by doing something meaningful for the society.

Many shine like bright stars on His horizon demonstrating divine grace to all His people. These stars are examples of His love. This boy is one such star used by God to spread His love to others.

1
Lost in the City

Trivandrum, Saturday evening, 12 March 1960. The state capital and the southernmost district of Kerala was abuzz with activity. And, it was the all-pervading commotion of this city which greeted Solomon.

Solomon, a young boy of 13, arrived in the city of Trivandrum, also called TVM City, from the neighbouring town of Colachel in Tamil Nadu by a government-owned state transport bus. The bus journey from his place to TVM city was about 60 kms and it cost him 50 paise. It was about six in the evening when he alighted from the bus. As he looked around himself, he could not hold back the flood of hot tears. He was in a state of distress. Helpless tears rolled down his smooth cheeks as he tried to get his incoherent thoughts together; many questions raced in his mind at that moment. He was absolutely at sea about what to do next. He had reached the city as he had initially planned, but what now? Fresh tears burst forth stinging his eyes. Where should he go from here? What should he do? There was no place or family he knew where he could stay; there was no one who might give him a morsel of food. He was hungry and desperately wanted a meal but had no idea of how and where he would get it. He was equally clueless about where he would spend the night. All around him he could only see unfamiliar faces, buildings and automobiles with dazzling headlights.

The city, which is the most populous city of Kerala, is the political nerve-centre of the state. In 1960, it was like one of the traditional cities of Kerala. It was slowly emerging into a metropolitan city, but was steeped in tradition and culture. It had charming old buildings with one or two high-rise buildings here and there; which were still a rarity then. The people still preferred the old, traditional style of architecture. Nothing significant was visible in the city's ambience and people's lifestyle. One could see more men in *veshtis* (men's clothing; dhoti) and many women wearing the traditional Kerala sari, *mundu-veshti*. The city was referred by Mahatma Gandhi as the 'Evergreen city of India'. It was characterized by its undulating terrain of low coastal hills and busy commercial alleys.

After an hour of pondering had passed, Solomon realized that he had come a long way from his home. His native place, Colachel, was a small town. It is a port on the Malabar Coast, almost 20 kms north-west of Kanyakumari, the southern tip of Peninsular India.

The place witnessed the battle between the Travancore forces led by King Marthanda Varma (1729–1758) and Dutch East India company forces led by Admiral Eustachius De Lannoy on 10 August 1741. It was the first time in Indian history that a European naval force was defeated by Indian forces. Colachel was home to about 10,000 families of mixed communities, whereas the city he had landed in had a head count of more than three lakh! There were vast differences in everything he saw around him. He could see the variance between his small hometown and this mega city with tens of thousands of families.

He deviated his mind away from the pressing questions about his survival in this mega city and started to spell out the differences between small villages and towns and big cities. There were wide gaps in infrastructural facilities such as the provision of drinking water, electricity, transport and medical services among villages, towns and cities.

Solomon had come from a municipal town which lies snugly close to the Bay of Bengal and had a small fishing yard. Since his street was little away from the centre, there was no water or power connection available in any of the houses in the street.

Politicians, bureaucrats, policy makers and planners, and even profit-mongering investors are interested in turning cities into mega centres for their own wealth creation. Even the government is keen to make our cities more attractive and investor-friendly to match with international standards in all respects rather than on rural infrastructure development. All seem to be worried about urban areas, creating places of tourist interest rather than upgrading rural areas from where our food baskets originate and sustain more than one billion people. The sooner the administration wakes up, the better it would be for the well-being of the nation. Though all these thoughts passed through the little mind, these things at the deeper level made no sense to him.

Solomon knew nothing about cities. Torn between his despair and the tell-tale landmarks of the mega city, he looked around to acknowledge the vistas that captured his sight. The regular commotion of a city was all around him; there were bus stands, railway station and a long line of shops with glittering lights.

His hometown did not have a railway station. He had never seen such a busy area where multitudes travelled, boarding and alighting by buses or trains. He had never before seen a city as busy as this with a plethora of shops, hotels, policemen, beggars and half-naked children, elderly women, men and invalids on the roadsides and the air buzzing with the noise of cars, buses, bikes, and bullock carts. All these made him apprehensive of the future days in store for him. How would he survive in this pressure-filled urban atmosphere?

The clock at the top of the railway station struck eight and sent his mind immediately racing back to the time at home. Were he at home now, he would have finished his supper and on some days, even gone to bed. At home, normally he and his family members together would have completed the night meal by 8 pm. He now felt hungry and thirsty. Never before in his life had he experienced hunger of this nature or magnitude. His stomach demanded its share of food. Hence, he decided to have a meal with the money he had.

Solomon crossed over to a nearby restaurant. This was the first time in his life that he was eating alone, away from home. As he ordered, he saw a young boy of about his own age serving the meal. What a tragedy! In the cities, children are serving as hotel servants instead of going to schools. He wondered why a small boy like him was engaged to work in the hotel. However, as soon as his meal arrived he stopped thinking of that boy. He felt happy about the meal and enjoyed it. Meals outside homes sometimes taste better! But in the long run they cause harm. Moreover, it cost him 25 paise. It was served on a table instead of the floor. Instantly, Solomon was reminded of his family and their habit of squatting on the floor when food was served. Painful memories of his family and home that he left for good returned dangerously. He missed the aroma of the delectable fish curry and garden-fresh vegetables that his mother cooked. There was no sharing of food among those present in the hotel. At home, everyone in the family ate together and most of the time everyone shared food. Also, they never wasted food. His mother always used to take the food in the last, after ensuring that everyone had eaten according to his need for the hour. His father always used to keep some morsel of food as leftover in his plate knowing that Solomon's mother would take that last morsel religiously. Solomon's young mind roved to the memories of his home and parents. Nostalgia hit him as he images of his family's happy and content faces as they sat down to dinner fleeted across his mind.

Ancient wisdom has it that families that pray together and eat together always stay together. Something extraordinary must have happened to young Solomon that he, much like a little deviant lamb in the flock, strayed away from his family. A moralist from a middle-class background may tend to label him as a 'black sheep' and write him off. But with divine grace Solomon was just a little lamb to be carried on the shoulder. But what forced him to leave his home, his family, and a carefree teenage life? Was he a rebel? Or was it his circumstances? These questions were difficult and hard to answer either for the members of his family or his friends.

The town from where Solomon had come was inhabited by families belonging to all faiths, cultures and value systems. There were more close-knit joint families than nuclear families. Everyone in a family had his/her own goal to pursue. However, most of the young ones wanted to be with their parents and other relatives. Many a youth of today wishing to meet their personal needs would embark on a journey outside the family fold wittingly or unwittingly and seek to settle down in a town or a city. Solomon took the decision as many as 50 years ago to leave his family and make the city his new home.

The city provides hardworking, enterprising youngsters with opportunities to succeed and prosper in life. Cities are increasingly becoming a place where genuinely hardworking persons can make wealth. Honest labour is duly rewarded. At the same time, one can also experience poverty, despair, inequalities, communal conflicts, and broken values. Life in a city is getting more dangerous these days. As the nation's population grows steadily, people are crowding into mega cities, where life's risks are horribly concentrated. Wanderers and waifs who stray aimlessly into a city are sure to fall into a rut and lead a subhuman life, totally unexpected and unwarranted. By the same token, the growth potential in the urban situation is also very strong which not only binds the families and communities together, but also makes civilization progress in rapid strides.

People, communities and nations are in a rat race to appropriate their portion of the wealth generated in the market. All the people born in this world have the space to operate in society, and depending upon their individual capacity can stake a claim to attain and live a good life. Nevertheless, the social fabric is strong in our culture. Hence, families and grassroots communities continue to maintain the ethos of love, affection, caring and sharing. In India, the family unit is somewhat strong and impresses visitors.

Solomon was haunted by memories of his family, his friends, school and the fresh air of the paddy field near his home. His tears would not stop. Realization hit him hard that he was after all a runaway lad from his home on account of a trivial reason. A boy from a good family, who was expected to sit for his final examination was now on the streets of Trivandrum city. The hope of pursuing his high school education stood shattered on the city road some 60 km away from his hometown. Who made the decision? What drove him to leave his secure home?

Our choices, not our chances, determine our density. People either become prosperous or mar growth and development purely by their thoughts and actions. Any decision taken by an individual of least influence affects only him and probably his immediate family. If a wrong decision is made by a person in authority, it brings incalculable damage to the community and even to the nation at times. But here an impulsive deviance in a 13-year old young boy to get out of an unpleasant situation back home landed him in deep distress. Could he not have avoided it? Had he debated various options available to him to get free from that mess, he would probably not have come this far. His remaining in this situation would indeed add on to the burden of the community and the nation. Sometimes people rush in where the angels hesitate to enter. But with divine grace, angels are posted to hold young ones like Solomon in their arms when they on an impulse jump down from the cliff.

Decisions, right ones and the not-so-right ones, rule our lives. This is one of the mysteries of the world. It gives a chance to historians to record for posterity the importance or the folly of decisions made by the rulers in a given context. By that time, enough damages would have been made and all the actors dead and gone. There is also a twist to the whole story. A runaway kid seldom makes it to the limelight as the streets always accommodate people, whether they belong to the high or low class. The universe never denies anyone the space he/she wants. Streets, city bridges, railway stations and bus stands are a home away from home for hundreds of boys and girls and their families.

A UN official estimate reports that more than 15 per cent of the world population lives on the streets. The figure for India may be about the same. It is a pity that India, which boasts of being on the frontline in the field of information technology, knowledge management and production is still not able to provide shelter to many millions both in rural areas and cities. Monsoon and cold weather in the winter in the northern areas claim many helpless lives every year and these lives are often those that are left to fend for themselves in the streets. Who is responsible for all disaster victims:

the policies of the country or the mindset of the rulers who never regard them as issues to address in their manifestoes? Are the people themselves to be blamed for electing such insensitive leaders to seats of power? Is it right on our part to leave these issues in the hands of God for solutions? Could we dismiss them off as low priority? For those of us who are blessed to have a roof above our head—a proper perfect hoe for ourselves—it is indeed difficult to stop to think of those who have no shelters whatsoever to call their own. The apathy towards the homeless is saddening. The plight of these living in the street is a bitter and terribly hurting.

Looking around at all the numerous options in front of him, and also keeping in account the paltry money that was secured in his pockets, Solomon decided that it was the best if he stayed the night at the railway station. For someone who had never ventured out of the warm embraces of his family, this indeed was a Herculean decision. The thought that he was no more a part of a well-knit family with reasonable living standards made him experience strong surges of regret regarding his decision to leave home. He felt unhappy about the circumstances which brought him to this situation and even cursed his fate. It is a tragedy of many a soul when the consequences of rash decisions are never for once pre-determined and judiciously presented. However, when the person usually faces the downfall and the aftermath, he feels distressed about it. The late self-realization will certainly not bring the required relief. One will be constrained to wait for ages to see the misdeed undone.

And Solomon cried bitterly. He had nobody to console him. Back home, whenever he cried one of his family members, father, mother or siblings had consoled him and condoned his wrong doings and sometimes even rewarded him with sweets! Now the scenario had completely changed. Worrying was not going to bring any solace to him. He had experienced love and care at home, but now there was no one to extend a helping hand. Having cried his eyes out, Solomon decided that it was indeed futile to cry over spilt milk. One thing that is agreed upon by a number of researchers and sufferers of stress alike is that wanting to cry and being unable to do so is disastrous. Hence shedding of tears acts as a safety valve to release stress. It was then that Solomon realized the need to be on his own in the city. Since he himself had made the decision to leave his family, there was no point in crying over that. Also, no one would understand his grief; neither would anyone bother about a small boy in the crowded platform of the busy railway station of this mega city. He also thought that if at all he wanted to survive, he should learn to relate to strangers in the city, befriend them and if possible love them and be loved by them. For a moment, he wondered who in a new city would love him, except God and therefore he decided that he ought to seek Him now more than ever.

"God. God will be there with me, I am sure."

2

Faith Triumphs Over Fear

Solomon hailed from a good Christian family; he never missed any of the Sunday church services, and went to Sunday school regularly. For some time, he was also a part of the church choir. Despite all these practices, he never truly realized the love of God. He went to the church regularly and attended services only because that was how Sunday began at home. All he knew till then was the love and affection of his parents and close family members. Of course, he also had a few good friends in school and in the community. But now that he was separated from everyone for the first time in his life, he started searching for love and affection outside his immediate circle of relations and friends. It also led him to think of God more. His mind went back to the debates that many boys had in school regarding the very existence of God and creation. The theory of creation as stated in the *Holy Bible* and the theory of natural evolution propounded by Charles Darwin were the topics of discussion during drill classes on the playground. In those days, during most periods of physical education and craft classes, children would be left free by the teachers concerned, who used the time to socialize with other teachers. The pupils found such free hours a welcome break to be on their own. The scenario has altered much today, where the students are subject to great strain, trapped in a tight schedule of study activities both during and after school hours.

Thanks to the free time that he was awarded at school along with other students, Solomon often chatted with his peers, raising random questions on the origin of the universe, creation, existence of God and so forth. But he was not much of a talker, rather he was a silent listener, perplexed with the dichotomy of varying ideas as to who was right: the Christian theologian or the scientist or other religious friends? This question will probably continue as long as men live on this planet.

Here now, for the first time in his life, Solomon faced the reality of the very existence of God and decided to put some faith in Him. He recognized the fact that if one puts his faith in others and sidelined God, then he was bound to fail because no human being was perfect. Faith in God, on the other hand, gave him stability of mind and peace. He acknowledged that God Almighty alone was perfect and would have a perfect plan for him as he did for every person on earth. This thought made him feel bold and confident, and gave him the strength to survive, though the knot of emotions was still raw in his throat and his eyes constantly misty. He could thus spend the night on the street on the first day of his self-imposed exile!

It was almost 9 pm. The busy bus stand and the railway station in the vicinity soon became quiet. The city was settling down for the night much earlier than one could visualize. The shop-fronts, which had been bright with lights and merchandise, were shut and dark. With curious eyes taking in every detail, Solomon looked around and saw vendors, casual labourers, travellers, and pedestrians soon disappearing. Even those who made their living on the street started looking for a place to lie down. The lucky ones found the benches in the railway station to stretch themselves. Some spread newspapers and towels on the floor to sleep on. A few others were late night shift workers who wanted to save on midnight travel to return home. Some were clubbers avoiding a long ride home. A sizable number were homeless, searching for safe places where they could doze off for a few hours. This, Solomon learned, was the other side of life in the cities. Many in their comfortable homes are oblivious to the plight of these people.

Solomon decided to lie down in a small corner of the railway station hall, considering it his home away from home. Prior to this, he tried to find a place to sleep in the nearby bus stand, but the place was already too crowded. Mostly people waited to catch the late night or early morning buses passing through or starting from the bus stand. Since he had landed just two hours before, he was very new to the situation and hence he could not find a place of his choice to sleep in the bus stand. He then decided to try his luck at the railway station. After a long search, he found a small place near the platform. The thought that someone might push him away from there, or worst, a police man would arrest him had in fact prevailed in his mind for a few moments but then he dismissed this as a useless thought and decided to sleep.

He was tired, his bones and every muscle of his body was strained to the hilt and were crying for some rest. But sleep decided to jilt him. God of Sleep failed to embrace him. He had no cot, no pillow and no bed sheet to protect him from the cold breeze. No order from father or mother directing the children to "Go to sleep!" All around him, there was only cement and stone floor, iron benches and strange people. He had never slept on the floor, that too without any pillow or bed sheet. He immediately thought of going back to home. But how could he go back? He had come a long way now. There were one or two people who had enquired about him. For everyone, he had one answer: "I came from the neighbouring town to see a movie, but I missed the bus and would catch the next day's early morning bus." This was the standard reply he decided to give whoever asked him as to how he came to be in the big city. He was restlessly tossing and eventually managed to sleep for a few hours despite the discomfort of the cement floor and the noise of the trains steaming in and out of the station.

When day broke, he got up much earlier than his usual time. There was no call from his mother directing him to have his coffee and study. There was also no call from his father and brothers indicating that it is morning and way past the time he should be up. At home, it was his duty to go to the nearby well to fetch water for various chores. This morning, he found himself relieved of that responsibility. Deviations in life provided opportunity to escape from responsibilities.

Solomon's first day at the city greeted him with the shrill sound of the steam engines leaving the station. He stretched himself gingerly, his bones aching from the contact with the bare cement floor all night. There was no familiar comforting aroma of coffee wafting in the air as at home. Instead of the voices of his parents calling out to him and his brothers, he heard some urchins squabbling over a packet of food left behind by a passenger. Solomon woke up to a new morning in the city, all alone, at the railway station. The station was bustling with activity, steam engines puffing away, the bogies clattering, the tea vendors and snack sellers calling out to passengers. He saw people entering the station. The daily commuters were busy finding their seats on the train. The occasional travellers were rushing to board the train. Not knowing what to do, Solomon sat there for a while, wondering where to go for a bath to freshen him up. After searching for some time, he found unclean toilets in the railway station and with great difficulty found a little space to freshen up. But then, he neither had any tooth powder nor soap to clean himself properly. Also there was no spare dress to change for the day. Slowly, he decided to go to the bus stand without knowing what course of action he should take next.

At the central bus stand, the scene was as crowded as it was at the railway station. People were running haphazardly to catch their buses. As usual, the coolies and daily wage earners stood conspicuously at the entrance looking for work. It has become a custom that daily wage earners usually come everyday in towns or cities to labour contractors, asking them to engage them in some work for a day or two. This practice, due to labour shortage, is now slowly becoming a thing of the past in many places.

The buses, all government-owned, were brightly coloured in red and orange. Kerala had a unique reputation for its state government-run public transport system. In fact, the people of Kerala wanted the government to play a major role in the public sector and opposed private ownership of property. This was a legacy of the Communist

Party. Kerala had the first elected Communist Government in the country in 1957. From the 50s through the 80s, the people of Kerala favoured public ownership of all the industries. They fought for individual rights and organized trade unions in all establishments. As a result, in those days many entrepreneurs shied away from setting up industries in the state. Even the little private industrialists always used to face labour trouble of one kind or the other. The very same Keralites who demand their due rights and do not hesitate to agitate for them when they are living in the state, become loyal and committed workers once they are out of it.. Being away from one's familiar terrain makes a person to mellow down on many fronts.

Solomon's normal day at home always started with a small personal prayer, reading a portion from the *Bible*, usual morning ablutions and then a cup of coffee. Thereafter, the house maintenance duties would begin, which were equally divided among the four brothers. While one was supposed to help in the kitchen, the other had to fetch water and the third one was given the responsibility to go to the local market to buy vegetables and fish for the day. The youngest of the four was spared from household duties all the time and he was called *chella pillai,* meaning affectionate son. After completing all the household duties, all the brothers would settle for an hour of study. Later, Solomon would go to the stream to take bath in the fresh water with his close friends. This was, in a sense, happy hour for the village boys where they would chat about school life, girls, boys, and teachers. During this hour, except on examination days, anything other than studies would be given top priority in discussion.

These thoughts reminded Solomon that today was his final examination for the eighth standard. Had he been home, he would have woken up much earlier and had an extra hour of study. Then it suddenly dawned on him that now no one would goad him to get ready and go to school! He had to look after himself from now on. Hereafter, he would be just one more person on the street. At that very moment, he thought of God and wondered what to do next. All mortals think about God and pray only when they are in trouble. In spite of his faith in God, Solomon was scared. From now on, he would be one among the millions in this city. He thought of Colachel where he was acknowledged to be an emerging leader in the school. It did not take him much time to realize that life was indeed a roller coaster ride now.

He wrestled with mixed feelings. He had two options—he could either stay in this huge, unfamiliar city and, with faith in God, look for a job, or could return home and be welcomed back by his parents with open arms. For a moment he thought that the latter would be the best option for him. However, there was a flip side to this option. He would be given a sound thrashing for missing from home for a good 18 hours. He pondered over his options thoughtfully.

Either stay on in this city and have a free life, or return home and be punished and then sent back to school after the summer holidays as if nothing had happened.

When faced with a dilemma, people always opt for the easier way out. They claim that they follow the dictates of their 'inner mind'. Conversely, a few take the hard option. Unfortunately, Solomon, who was faced with an unpleasant situation in life, also took the hard option, to run away from home, instead of facing the situation and getting excused or punished by his parents for his extravagant life. In fact, that would have solved the entire issue.

Since there was no other way out, Solomon decided to stay on in this alien city, absolutely unaware of its repercussions. But one thing was clear: from now on the journey would be a far cry from the comfortable and carefree life that he had at home. This decision could end up making him a street fighter or smuggler or a porter or he may even become a politician or an underworld criminal! Or he could perhaps end up being a beggar on the street or a Robin Hood! What he was not prepared for was the physical discomfort, the emotional turmoil, the agonizing thoughts, and the feelings of sorrow, guilt, frustration and failure.

Solomon was feeling quite ravenous by now. He felt the coins in his pocket and knew he had to use them judiciously. He went out of the railway station and discovered that there were many small restaurants which catered to the transit passengers, new arrivals to the city, and those who lived and worked in the vicinity. Since he was unfamiliar with Malayalam, he hesitantly asked for some *idlis* and *sambar* at the first restaurant. The man behind the counter was tearing out little colour-coded coupons, indicating a particular dish which one got after making the payment. Solomon got one too, a pink coloured one indicating *idli* and *sambar*. He went to the service-counter and handed over the coupon to the man behind it. The man yelled out his order along with the many other orders of other customers for *idli* or *vada* or *Malabar parotta*, which is typical of Kerala, or *idiappams*, which are light and stringy like vermicelli but made of rice flour, or *masala dosa*, to the persons working in the hot steamy kitchen. The cook ladled out the portion onto a plate and placed it on the ledge of the window between the kitchen and the service-counter. The man at the service-counter took the plate and handed it to Solomon, who walked carefully back to a table to sit.

Solomon dipped a piece of *idli* into the steaming *sambar* and popped it in his mouth. The steaming hot *idli* and the *sambar* scalded his tongue. It was not the same as his mother's fluffy and soft *idlis*, and he found the *sambar* a little bland for his taste. Nevertheless, it was food, and it was hot and filling. Although he felt very homesick before and while eating his breakfast, he felt better after he finished. He walked back to the railway station and sat in a corner of the entrance, thinking about his next step. Solomon had lasted the night and had managed to see through the morning. His

Christian upbringing and church impartation, and faith and hope in the Lord stood him in good stead. Fear and faith cannot coexist any more than light and darkness can. To overcome fear, one must have faith. For the boy, it seemed faith had triumphed over fear.

3

First Earning

Boys and girls who have to live on the street are either orphans or runaway vagabonds. In North American parlance, they are labelled as 'lazy bums'. Of late, however, professional social workers refer to them as 'street children'. Most people who come across these children in the streets dismiss them as destitute and drop a few coins in their hands as an expression of sympathy or pity. Street children working and living on the streets, in parks and pavements, bus stations, railway stations, and other public places are actually without safety and security.

Most of them have parents and in a few cases a single parent. According to a recent study, the majority have their own families either in their native places or in the cities where they live. They leave their home for varied reasons and seek a livelihood outside the warmth of their families. A few are found to be from reasonably well-to-do families. They might have run away from home and from their familiar environment as something untoward might have happened in the family or school. A few (the minority) end up in the streets, as a result of rebellion against the traditional authority of elders at home or as a reaction to some disciplinary measure in the family. Most of these kids are from the lowest strata of the society who come to cities in the hope of making a living. Solomon, however, came from a well-to-do family, and was now a street child.

Days went by and Solomon defied his own thoughts and resisted the urge to return home. He was not sure as to how many days he would continue to live on the streets of Trivandrum. He spent his time sitting alone either at the bus stand or the railway station, walking up and down, reading papers and magazines left by the passengers. He realized that he was running out of money. So, he ate sparingly, often going on an empty stomach. All the while, he was keenly aware that somebody from his native district might recognize him. A few of the 'platform sleepers', who enquired about him, found that he belonged to a decent family and had left his home. They took pity on him and advised him to go back. One of the elderly among them started sharing some food with him. Solomon learnt that there is always caring and sharing among the poor once they understand each other.

Time continued its monotonous journey and after living in the streets for four days, Solomon found himself in a deplorable condition; he was dirty, his hair was neither clean nor oiled or groomed. He looked like a street beggar. What a fall from grace and love that his parents showered on him at home! No one ever looked at him, let alone speak to him. He was still not sure whether the decision taken by him was correct or not. He now calculated his 'net worth' in monetary terms; he was left with seven rupees. During the last few days, he had spent six rupees. Apart from those seven rupees, his prized possessions included a prestigious 'Pilot' pen which was gifted to him by his grandfather when he reached the eighth standard. He always kept this with him.

Solomon wore a simple dress—shorts and a multi-coloured shirt. Those were all his worldly possessions. He had just about enough money to see him through with food for another 10 days or so. The fact that he was extremely poor suddenly sank in. Solomon cried bitterly till tears refused to come out any more. Till a few days back, he was a child who was loved by everyone in his family, who had many friends to play with, and hot delicious food to dig his hands into. And now, no one even looked at him, let alone love!

Whenever he was thirsty, the water taps at the railway station allowed him to quench his thirst. That was in the earlier days the only natural wealth available to the people as free commodity. In those days, one could see people running with empty utensils to fetch water from the station taps or from the bathrooms of the railway wagons. Today water has become such a precious commodity that it has become the bone of contention between nations. In fact, a continuous supply of water at a particular site or area was the origin for many of our civilizations. However, millions all over the world are deprived of clean drinking water.

What happened to all the theories which our planners and administrators formulated in economics with regard to pricing of commodities based on the cost of production? Who is responsible for our farmers remaining constantly at subsistence level? The results of these injustices are that many in the villages are forced to give up their traditional occupations and migrate to the cities. Thus there are pockets of migrant population in the city slums unwittingly contributing to the squalor and social degradation. Children and youth, like our runaway lad in Trivandrum, are sure to be exposed to a severely devalued lifestyle.

At the railway station, the cement bench, the common water tap and the free-for-all public toilets were Solomon's miniscule world. The day's life unfolded to him as a day of hard work, full of struggle to get enough to eat. One day, as he sat on his haunches on the platform, he thought about the dwindling rupees in his pocket and knew he had to do something and soon! He watched the urchins who would collect bits and pieces from the heaps of garbage scattered around the railway station. But he could not bring himself to rummage in the filth as a ragpicker.

He then saw some boys, some as old as himself, carrying the luggage of the passengers. He decided to give it a try. He looked at the great mounds of bags piled up on the platform and balked at the prospect of carrying so much. He saw an old lady who had a small suitcase. He thought he would be able to lift it without much difficulty and went towards the lady. However, before he could reach her, another boy was quicker and the lady gave her suitcase to that boy with relief. Solomon stood there, bitterness welling up inside him.

Just then, a train from erstwhile Madras or Chennai, as it is known now, steamed unto the platform. Solomon ran along the train on the platform as it slowed down before coming to a halt. He knew he had to be quick to get to a passenger who did not have too much luggage. He saw a small family of three getting down from a bogie. The woman was carrying a baby in her arms and her husband had two suitcases in his hands. Solomon ran towards them and heard the familiar cadences of Tamil. He asked the woman, "*Amma*, may I carry your suitcase?" The woman smiled at him on hearing Tamil and turned to her husband. The man with the suitcases gave the smaller of the two to him and signalled to him to follow him. Solomon struggled to keep up with the man's long strides while the metal handle of the suitcase bit into his palm. The woman followed some distance behind him, trying to rock the baby who was getting more and more restless.

Outside the railway station, there was a group of cycle rickshaw drivers, jostling each other and calling out to the passengers. The man spoke to one of the cycle rickshaw drivers and then gestured to his wife to hurry up. He then looked around for Solomon who was just behind him and nodded to him to follow him. On reaching the cycle rickshaw, Solomon placed the suitcase on it, his fingers making a painful claw when he let go of the handle because he was not used to lifting so much of weight. He waited while the man took out a few coins and handed them over to Solomon. Solomon looked at the coins glistening in the sun—ten paise! His first earning! His fingers ached as he carefully stashed them away in his pocket. This was a beginning, he thought.

He made it a habit of commuting between the bus stand and the railway station, which was hardly about 500 metres looking for the job of a coolie or a porter. If he was lucky enough, he would get one or two customers to carry their bags and would get anywhere between 5–10 paise for the load. Sometimes, he was engaged by passengers to carry things to their home and then he would get little extra. However, there was hardly any time when he was paid more than 15 paise for a trip with load.

At home, whenever his paternal uncle visited their home, the boy used to carry his small bag to the bus stand

and his uncle used to give him 25 paise as a token gift plus some snacks and tea at the small tea-shop near their house. Now, even for a long distance, with load as heavy as himself, he was paid less than 10 paise! Earning a few coins had become a big struggle whereas there were times in the past when he used to spend money, in the form of notes and not coins!

In those days, a meal cost 25 paise. There were days when Solomon got more than 25 paise and such days were blessed days as he could ensure a meal or two and could even save some for peanut cake and plantain. Nevertheless, most of the days, he failed to get even 25 paise which resulted in going to bed on an empty stomach. On such days, peanuts provided him the required nourishment. The days when he went to sleep without a full meal were torturous days for young Solomon. He could not sleep. Instead, he would imagine that one day he would either become a dreaded criminal on the street with nefarious behaviour or become a great man. Whatever it may be, Solomon found himself in vulnerable position.

It amazed him how quickly he had come to terms with his new situation and adjusted to it. At that point in time, he was not mature enough to grasp life's lessons. But over the years, he learnt that life always offers opportunities to everybody. It was left to each individual to weigh the pros and cons before making a decision. Whatever that decision may be, one should be firm and move forward with courage and confidence. There are sure to be risks, but cultivating faith in God and confidence in one's own worth can see one through several crises.

God has endowed all people with great talents to cope with the pleasant as well as the unpleasant facets of life. Despite socio-economic deprivation, devastation due to natural calamities, riots and social upheavals, people somehow get over these crises and advance in life hoping for light at the end of the dark tunnel. Two weeks had passed since Solomon had left home. Whatever money he had was all spent within one week and the second week was spent mostly by living on his small earnings. One day, when his extravagant self took the better of him, he went to watch a movie. At home, he occasionally went to watch films with his friends and family. It was the hugely successful Malayalam movie, *Chemmeen*, a true love story of a boy and girl from two different communities of Kerala.

In the south, as in the rest of the country, movies hold a special fascination for the youngsters. In the 60s, it was more so because this was much before the era of television and other means of entertainment. The mesmerizing influence of cinema also saw the rise of popular cine stars in the field of politics. The release of a new film featuring their favourite actor would have his fans in a frenzy. They would form numerous fan clubs. It was not uncommon to see enormous cut-outs of the actors with flower garlands around their necks, placed reverentially by their fans. The rivalry between the respective fans of the stars would often turn violent, with each group claiming that their idol was superior. The characterization played out on celluloid would be carried in the minds of those who came to watch the films and many would emulate the mannerisms. There were some who would try and replicate the exploits which they saw in the crime thrillers with tragic consequences. It was a three-hour fantasy world, their own Disneyland, where they laughed and cried with those on the screen and clapped and rejoiced when the villain staggered up to the hero and blabbered his apology and was led away by the police into the final fade-out of the frame.

Solomon was no different; he settled back into his seat and lost himself in the story unfolding before his eyes. He wondered about the emotions of the characters as he was still too young to understand the intensity of the emotion of love, however that did not come in way of his enjoying the film. The film flickered to an end and Solomon slowly walked out of the cinema hall. It was a treat he had given himself after a long time. Slowly, the reality of his situation crept back in and the euphoria dripped away from him as the rivulets of perspiration down his thin body. With all his money spent, it became very hard to get enough work and money, and a feeling of despair set in. He again thought of going back home. Nevertheless, the betrayal he had inflicted on his family was too much to bear and there was no way he could now undo it. The present reality had to be faced somehow. He could not go back home for now, but build his life from scratch right here on the street. His priority for the time being then was to get a job so that he could get at least a square meal a day.

To achieve positive results in life, one must always nourish positive feelings and positive thoughts. The habits which children pick up when young, in most cases, stay with them even when they grow up. Parental care and home discipline should aim at imparting moral values: love, humility, respect for family, faith in God, and prayer and devotion which alone will stand in good stead. These will blossom and yield fruit in due season.

4

Life as a Street Urchin

Days turned into weeks and Solomon continued to make his living on the railway platform, alternating between the bus stand and the railway station. There was no sign that his family was looking for him. Had they all forgotten him? Would they have consciously disowned him? It dawned on him that for a family of their social standing, his disappearance from home would have been a cause of much embarrassment and dishonour in their circle of friends and relatives and in the neighbourhood. As he ruminated on the present situation, he saw himself not as a teenager, childish and immature, but as a grown up, capable of independent thinking and acting. Where there is a will there is a way, he reminded himself and resolved that he would never go back home again. Certainly not now when he thought that his family and friends did not seem to miss him at all. Maybe his parents had decided that the other three sons were enough. He felt that the others in his hometown would have missed him for a while and then forgotten about him. If he returned now, he was sure he would be shown the door.

His thoughts went to his friends. Had they all too forgotten him? What about his best friend Bhasker, who studied with him and was his companion for seven years from the second class onwards? Bhasker and Solomon always made it a point to spend about 10 minutes together before the class started, mulling over the previous day's happenings. They were seen together during the breaks between classes. They always spent time cycling together, at times bunking their classes during the last hour, especially from the sports period. During the lunch break, they sat in the nearby mango garden, chatting about sundry things. Life was so peaceful and carefree then. What about his other friends? Had they also forgotten him? He recollected the memories of good days as well as bad. But thoughts about his best friend Bhasker continued to play in his mind.

Solomon and Bhasker had enacted the role of best friends even on stage in a school play. It was the story of X and Y who hailed from a remote village. As children, they loved each other and spent most of their time together. They grew up to be very close friends, loving and caring for each other. When they became adults, they parted and moved on to live in different places. Y travelled to a far off country where he was arrested for a major offence. The king of that land pronounced him guilty and sentenced him to death. Hearing this, X made his way to the king's court to plead his friend's case. He meets Y in the jail. Excited to meet his friend, Y shared his desire to visit his village and bid goodbye to his people before his impending death. X offered to stay in prison while Y went to his village to bid everyone a final goodbye. X met the king and negotiated that if Y did not return in 10 days, he could be sent to the gallows instead. The day for the public hanging came and there was no sign of Y. As the clock ticked away, it was decided that X would be sent to the gallows. Just as the hangman was about to tighten the noose round X's neck, there is a shout from the crowd, "Stop! Stop!! Stop!!!" It was Y pushing his way through the crowd to save his friend in the nick of time. The story ended with the king decreeing the release of both the friends, moved by their true friendship.

In that play, Solomon played the role of X, while Bhasker played Y. But what happened to that friend now? Was he indeed a true friend as in the story? Solomon wondered if Bhasker would have attempted coming to the city in search of him. If Bhasker had come, he probably would have brought some news about his family, and depending on the news, Solomon could have determined his next move. Or if Bhasker should choose to join him, they both could open a new chapter in their lives. Life would then have turned into an adventure with added strength and support. He was again plagued by doubts. Was Bhasker just a fair-weather friend and nothing more? Did friendship continue only as long as there was mutual admiration and common interest? Should it disappear once the two went to different life pursuits, taking them physically away from each other? If theirs was true friendship, then did it break only because he left home?

Solomon had now come to the conclusion that he was a useless soul as no one seemed to be bothered about him and no one missed him. It seemed to him that nothing in life was permanent, except the love of God. He remembered what he had read in his Moral Science textbook: "To have friends, be a friend. To be remembered, remember others. To be loved, love." With that feeling, he tried to relate to the persons he met in the present situation. He made friends with other boys who had made the streets their home. A few grown-ups had also befriended him. They would tease him about the way he spoke the local language, Malayalam. He did some menial jobs for them when they wanted. In the street community, no one, especially the younger ones, could afford to displease the older people. All said and done, for those with little or no money, life on the street was one of pain and agony.

Most of the other street boys were rag pickers who eked a living out of the garbage dumped on the street. They rummaged through all the waste and collected used paper, bottles, and plastics. They would then sell them for throwaway prices for their living. On rainy days, they struggled even harder. For several days, they had to manage with only one meal a day. Sometimes the boys in the streets used to collect almost rotten fruits and other waste food stuffs. Few very gladly took them as the manna of the day. Occasionally, Solomon was also offered these stuffs by other boys, but then he hesitated to accept them. If at all he took what was offered to him, he would take a bite and throw it where it belonged. This obviously did not go down too well with the other boys and they thought it a trait of bad behaviour on the part of Solomon. However, later they realized that he was not able to stomach this food which was so different from that he was used to at home. They were used to all this but Solomon could only blame himself for not being able to eat what the others ate.

Solomon and even those who live on the streets used to see all the wealth and pomp displayed by others before their poverty-stricken eyes. Being deprived of the physical comforts and unable to fulfil their wants, they felt very frustrated. At times like these, the elders from the group became judgemental and questioned as to why God has allowed the people to be sharply divided into the 'haves' and the 'have-nots'. Their discussions would often led them to the conclusion that most people do not recognize or do not want to recognize the fact that such a division is man-made; it is caused by man's exploitative nature, seeking to satisfy his greed for money and material things. Greed gives rise to all kinds of anti-social activities. Ultimately, it is the situation of not having enough to meet even the basic needs that lead to unlawful acts.

Solomon now realized the urgent need to look for some job as there was no money left with him. One or two of his friends on the street were employed in nearby shops and hotels. He wanted to be employed either as a server in a hotel, or as a sales boy in a shop, or as a petty porter at the railway station. His mind was not ready to accept any other job at that point of time. He did not like the idea of rummaging through garbage for a small income. The boys in the street used to collect old papers, plastics, bottles, etc., from the dumped waste and sell them in the nearby junk shops and would thus make an income. He thought that this would be the worst job and felt that no one should be driven to such a state. He did not see any difference between a stray dog which feeds on stale waste food and a street boy who does the same for a living. He also saw the despair of the boys who were engaged in rag picking. But if nothing should come his way, he realized he too would have to resort to rag picking. Such thoughts chilled him to the bone. He prayed to God that he be spared such a fate.

He felt the need to have a pen and to buy Tamil magazines, to be informed of the latest stories in the print media. Incidentally, the 'Pilot' pen, which he held on to as his precious possession, was taken by one of his street 'seniors' when he was asleep. He also lost a few coins which he had carefully saved for the next day's meal. When he questioned the others, they feigned ignorance. For the first time, he realized the futility of attaching importance to possessions as wealth would not accompany one always. On the other hand, acts of kindness to others shall merit recognition and appreciation.

Since Solomon was from a middle class family, whenever his grandparents visited his home, they used to give some spare money to him and his brothers. While his brothers always saved the money for spending during the festival time, Solomon would immediately spend his share. He was under the impression that one man's expenditure was other man's income. Most often than not, these small tips were spent on making others more happy, especially the poor and his fellow classmates. Some of his schoolmates used to go without food during the lunch time. Occasionally, Solomon used to not only spare some food from his basket for those boys, but very often he was found in nearby eateries with his friends. The boys would be ravenous and would finish off everything with great gusto. He found lunch break to be an ideal time to spend with friends.

Slowly, the habit of eating out with friends became a permanent feature. However, whatever meagre amount he got was never enough for them all. The idea of spending time with friends and also eating food in the small eateries ensnared Solomon; the lure of fast food or junk food was as much present as now, albeit in a different form. It was so strong that he even started stealing few coins from his home without anybody's notice. He also started borrowing from other boys who hailed from better-off family background. He started the art of borrowing and repaying. Savings and credit did exist among few boys in the school. Later still, as if this was not enough, Solomon was also drawn towards cycling. But since he did not have a cycle of his own, he started borrowing money from his friends to hire a bicycle during lunch hours and display his skills in cycling. At first, Solomon, like other boys, never thought that these habits would deviate him from his studies, but then slowly, all these extravagant habits and lack of foresight, which was due to his immaturity, ended up in him borrowing more and more money from fellow students and then resorting to some foul play to pay back the money. This continued for some time and Solomon's days were filled with playing with his friends without much thought or care; until one day, all his doings caught up with him. Solomon, who should have been on summer holidays with friends enjoying every moment in sports and other activities, found himself alone on the streets of a city nearly as a beggar. Whether it was fate or God's own mysterious way to teach him a lesson, Solomon wondered, but never got an answer.

One day a rather well-dressed and good-looking railway passenger hired Solomon to carry his luggage to his home which was a kilometre away. With great difficulty, Solomon lifted the bag, carried the load, and reached the passenger's home, while the well-dressed man strutted in front. After reaching, Solomon expected a substantial wage. He at least deserved more than 50 paise for he had carried that heavy load all the way from the station to this man's house. Naïve Solomon had already decided that he would first go and watch a movie and with the remaining money, he would eat a hearty meal. But as luck would have it, he was paid not even half the amount he had expected. When he pleaded for more, the man's face turned dark with anger and he threatened Solomon who cowered away in fear. This was the first incident which introduced young Solomon to the omnipresent phenomenon of exploitation of labour by the rich and the powerful. Being of a small stature and also not familiar with the local area and people, Solomon had to suppress his feelings of distress and anger. He could experience but not react to the reality of how street children were unfairly treated and exploited by others. Exploitation of the most vulnerable by the most powerful is common in our society. But what could a poor boy do under the circumstances? He could only put the blame on his fate and told himself that the amount paid would at least ensure a full meal.

For a moment, his mind flashed back to his classroom. One day during the history period, the teacher had touched on topics such as division of labour, wages, capital, and Karl Marx. To most of the boys, all these topics then sounded like fairy tales from history. Few rich boys thought that the teacher was against their families and hence they purposely talk about labour class, land lord, etc. Solomon, like most other boys, took it as lessons for examination and not for life. He also recollected the history teacher talking about the industrial revolution in England, the aftermath of inhuman conditions of labourers engaged in factories, and the subsequent labour welfare measures initiated by the British Parliament. All these lessons which sounded as fairy tales then, now struck on Solomon's face as real life melodrama. He could now see in front of his own eyes many from the labour class, especially the porters and construction workers living in the city, without proper shelter and food. There were no sanitary facilities. The earnings were not sufficient to make both ends meet.

He just concluded that one day his life would change for better. He also thought that the rich should not be arrogant and put their hope in wealth, which is uncertain. Instead, the rich and the more powerful should find ways and means to help the 'have-nots' and things will soon change. He also learnt his first lesson from the low wage he received—to survive on the street, one needs to indulge in all kinds of bad behaviour. Falsehood, covetousness, abuses, threats, violence, cheating, oppression; the list seemed endless. More so, one should be more vocal in demanding. He learnt in those few days that life on the street was an institution in itself. He also learnt that he had to be as hard as a nail to survive on the streets. He knew now that it was going to be impossible for him and for others like him, who lived on the street, to lead a clean life. If they were to depend on their street peers for a living, comradeship, and company, they would certainly land in trouble. No matter how difficult it was going to be, getting a job was of paramount importance. He realized the seriousness of it all and did not want to be privy to street vices. He started to look for a steady income-fetching job. He enquired in a number of shops for a job. Though they all pitied him, none of them offered him one.

Thanks to his upbringing, he resolved that he would not knowingly break the law. However, he lacked the force of conviction to urge him on in his quest to find a job. Strangely, his courage to face the hard realities of life seemed to fail him each day, though he had the determination to carve out a life for himself. He often thought of committing suicide by throwing himself on the railway track under a speeding train. But sheer fright or maybe the fear of a gruesome death held him back. Also, he was scared that he might just become a cripple instead of dying. This would make him dependent on others—the last thing that he wanted. He certainly did not wish to live a life of poverty, begging for alms and existing on charity. This fear in him indeed was very real and genuine.

The other more perplexing and daunting fear preventing him from attempting suicide was about the fate of his soul once he breathed his last. Raised in Christian faith, he remembered the exhortations of the parish priest and his mother about the soul being destined for eternal life. He also remembered the time when Cherian, a young man living close to his house, had ended his life because of some problem. Cherian's family could not bury him in the cemetery; the words of his mother still echoed in Solomon's ears, "Pah! That Cherian! How could he do this to his mother? It is bad enough he is dead. But the sin! He will rot in hell. His family has to face the shame of burying him in unconsecrated ground. Now who will marry Omana?" Solomon did not want his family to be shamed further. He did not want to rot in hell like the late lamented Cherian. He believed that his soul would travel to the very presence of God the moment he ceased to exist on this earth. But because of his disturbed state of mind and the lack of spiritual fervour to seek the presence of God through regular prayers, he began recollecting scary thoughts about spirits of the deceased hovering around, as his mind went back to what his English teacher in school once recounted in class.

One day, his teacher kept her pupils spell-bound with her narration of the journey of the soul after death. The human soul, after leaving the body, she told her young students, would continue to be in the atmosphere of its familiar territory. It wandered around its loved ones on earth. Then it would go higher into the clouds and to heaven or be plummeted down to depths closer to hell. It would then decide to be reincarnated and become a human life again by entering into a newborn baby. Thus it would start a new life on earth. This teacher held the view that all unfulfilled desires and aspirations in the earlier life would come to pass in the new life, provided the soul in its previous life had done good deeds. Further, the teacher told the class that reincarnation depended upon one's good deeds or bad deeds. Therefore, she would exhort them to follow the principle of doing good to others all the time in order that their souls were duly rewarded in the next birth.

The idea of his becoming an invalid for life or assuming a much less satisfying life in the next birth held him back. Many who decided to end their lives might not have been told, nor would they have had an English teacher to warn them about life after death. For a young class that was probably hearing about life after death for the first time, this was very interesting and inspired contemplation of a new spiritual pursuit. The teacher happened to know Solomon and his family personally. So she took all the trouble to convince him to be good in studies by ensuring that his life was built on the principles and values his family stood for. God is truly good and always kind to all, irrespective of their colour, race, religion and capabilities. He draws them back to Himself, which is why His love is amazing and marvellous. However, this philosophy of reincarnation confused Solomon because he had been taught that all souls had to wait for Judgment Day after the soul left the body. There was no concept of rebirth or doing or undoing deeds of a past life; instead, there was only one life that was taken into account. The thoughts heaven and hell were far from Solomon's mind at this juncture. His young mind was plagued by thoughts of the lurking spirits and ghosts and the horror of being crippled for life because of a foolhardy step of suicide. Young Solomon had not bargained for the burden of these thoughts when he ran away from home. He was growing up very fast indeed!

5

Surviving on Streets

Human beings need to be under the mentorship of a good teacher. In the absence of a teacher, there may be another elder or preacher who can mould young minds and sensitize them to social realities while imparting them the courage to do good and overcome evil. Thanks to his strong foundation in Christian faith, laid so firmly by his parents, especially his devoted mother, Solomon did not succumb to his teacher's philosophy. He was convinced that with death the soul ceased to live in the mortal body. It would pass into eternity, which was an entirely different realm, under the total control of Almighty God.

However, sometimes his mind was preoccupied not with any religious beliefs or tenets of philosophy, but only with thoughts of whether he should end his life or not. Although he had allowed his mind to reflect on another philosophy, his roots in Christian faith restrained him from yielding to the soul reincarnation theory. He had not lived a concrete life yet to give a proper account. So he convinced himself that he was not ready to meet God yet. He thought that he would make his life worthwhile on earth by simply trusting His guidance. Though death seemed to be an easy answer, he did not want it. He was not a coward. Though he ran away from home, he could not run away from facing life. He had it in his mind and heart to try and attempt making his life rather than breaking it. Heroism and a mindset for solving problems were his inherent strengths. As long as he had these coupled with his unshakable and quiet faith in God, he was not going to give up. He set forth in his business of locating an appropriate job, whereby to work, earn and live independently.

He relied on the strength and support he received from God, and looked upon the days to come with fresh hope. Everyone on this planet has a space and right to live, and therefore all should live and let others live. Living only for oneself should not be one's life goal, but it should involve helping others in similar or worse situations. It is God's will that each one of us is born in a particular family, not of our choice but His. But within the limited sphere of social standing, one should strive to serve others. This thought was planted in Solomon's mind as leaven in the dough by the teachings of his mother and the sermons he heard every week.

While creating simple things like drawing or painting or even making a pot from clay, many of us would assign a specific purpose to that product's end use. If mortals can apply so much of their minds and think of making something great with a meaning or a purpose, how much more would the Creator have considered before creating the universe. As such, by creating human beings, God had a purpose, which He spelt out in His call to serve our neighbours in need. Solomon thought that there was some purpose behind his running away from home and that God had willed it. He decided that he would now look for work, full-time or part-time; any work that he can lay his hands on.

If today, a child of 13 sought work, there would be few takers as there is social sanction against child employment. Until some years ago, child labour was not considered such a big issue. Till recently, when the law came into full effect, many preferred to engage children for odd jobs as they could work long hours, and be paid much less than adults without any fear of retaliation. However, although there were no restrictions, there were very few jobs. Even today, there are children who are unfortunately burdened with responsibilities of providing for their family needs right from the age when they ought to be in primary school.

These children find it difficult to find work or are exploited by their employers. It is not unusual to find an odd kind-hearted employer who is aware of the law but philosophizes that if the child did have an option, then he would not be working, so better that the child was working for him rather than starve, or worse, get into nefarious activities. There are no easy answers.

Having resolved to make a living, Solomon offered to work as a porter at the railway station and the bus stand. Each trip fetched him about 10 paise and sometimes even 15. His regular visits to and from the station and bus stand helped him make acquaintance of a few families that lived nearby. He frequently went to their homes to do odd jobs like going to the market, getting pulses, gram and dried chillies, or even carrying firewood and storing them in their homes. Back in the 50s and until the 80s, many hotels and houses used only firewood for cooking purposes. In rural areas, in addition to the firewood, dried cow dung was also used as an energy source. Now things have changed as electricity and gas are in use.

Compared to others, since Solomon was new to the trade, he never demanded anything in addition to what they usually paid him. Whatever they gave was graciously accepted as the best reward for his work. He was not aware then that he was being underpaid. Poor labourers were and even now are exploited in the market by others because of their politeness and also because they never demanded their due for the work done.

Since he hailed from a good family with religious values, Solomon always displayed good behaviour when dealing with others. Also, when a few families employed him, they used to give him some leftover snacks besides money as wages. One family even asked him to be the in-charge of their cattle, but Solomon politely refused. Had he accepted, he would have probably become a cattle merchant. Whenever he received these snacks that were now precious delights, he remembered how these were available in plenty at his grandfather's home. But then they, he and his brothers, never relished. When they visited their grandfather, and their aunts or grandmother gave them snacks to eat, the children would make a fuss over what they got and ate very little of it. They would run off in their excitement to play outside. What he had earlier wasted was now priceless to him. It is often said that one does not realize the value of things until one loses it. There is a time for everything, time to reject and time to accept the very same things gracefully! Whenever things come free or easily, people have no value for it. On the other hand, if they have to pay even something meagre to obtain it, then they realize its importance. This is true even of love, affection and care. Even a good meaningful act of charity is either questioned or doubted.

Several weeks had gone by and Solomon's only objective was day-to-day survival. This was true for most boys who made streets their home. Their goal was also survival, getting a minimum of 25 paise everyday so that they could buy some food. In Trivandrum, they could get a full meal in the night for 25 paise. There were days when he earned extra and it would be spent on ground nut sweets and plantains. There were days when he could not even get 25 paise, leaving him to live on tea, nuts and plantains only. On the contrary, today it is widely believed that beggars in cities do not want to accept any coin of lower denominations. They tend to demand or bargain for alms of higher value. It is reported that some beggars even have cellular phones in their hands in cities like Mumbai and Delhi. There was a recent report that a beggar had accumulated lakhs which were discovered in his post office accounts. However, these are far and few between and the condition of the people who have to live on the streets is indeed heart-rending.

Solomon's peers, when they met after a hard day's work, enquired more and more about his family background as he did not show any sign of going back home or reveal anything about himself to others. Nor was he ready to do the most 'menial' job of picking from the trash cans. During his life on the street, he noted that a few newcomers were from Tamil Nadu. However, most of them, after spending just a few days, suddenly disappeared from the street. But Solomon was different. There was a reason for his reticence. He was not yet at ease with the local language and yet he did not want anyone to identify him as an outsider. Should his manner of speaking betray him, he might lose his right to live on the streets of Trivandrum. Moreover, he did not want anyone to inform his whereabouts to his parents or relatives. He was not quite ready for that. Therefore, he always kept a low profile. Whether he really liked staying on the street, or whether something compelled him to continue his life in this city was a mystery to everyone.

Solomon continued to slog on the streets of Trivandrum and thought that he would spend the rest of his life in the same way. He had become a junior porter like in the railway station. This seemed to be the best job he could manage to get. He did not express the pain he was suffering. At the railway station, porters were at the mercy of the passengers. Though the railway station had many porters, they had to accept whatever the passengers gave as 'coolie' meaning 'service charge'. On the contrary today, porters everywhere demand high 'coolie' and somehow extract it from the travellers. In big railway stations, even before the train comes to a halt, porters jump into the compartments, then lift the pieces of luggage with utmost care and bring them on to the platform. In the ensuing bargain, they demand exorbitant amounts to carry the luggage. Today, passengers end up paying much more than the official rates.

Solomon occasionally thought of his home, relatives, friends and school mates. His thoughts went out to his school where he used to perform well in extra-curricular activities and won the appreciation of one and all. But even as he fondly reminisced about his home and family, he never had the courage to board a bus to return to his people. It would have cost him only 50 paise which he could have made by skipping two meals. That would have taken him back to his old comfort. Or even a post card to his parents, informing them of his whereabouts would have solved all the problems. But he stopped short of taking that step. Most often, we hesitate to make that crucial decision for fear of the outcome about which we are not certain. People usually complicate matters by not taking appropriate action at the right time. They have a tendency to procrastinate and, in the process, become very indecisive. They also hesitate to take the first step to progress as they perceive risks in it. But to succeed in life, one needs to be focussed in one's aims and aspirations. One should direct his entire energy towards achieving the goal. Many fail to do this. If success does not come their way, they blame God for their plight.

Nevertheless, what prevented Solomon from returning home is a mystery. Probably, he thought it would be better to return home with a lot of money, sporting a tag of being a self-made man which would justify his running away. To succeed in life, whatever be the circumstances, one must work hard. One should not focus only on the obstacles, but must try finding ways and means to deal with them and overcome them. One must be aggressive and persevere in one's efforts. Throughout history, we see many instances of those who left their home for a livelihood and have made fortunes by their sheer dedication, determination, diligence and hard work. Of course, there may be a few others who ended up as roadside vendors, casual labourers, and some even as street rowdies, criminals, smugglers and pimps.

Sometimes he remembered his mother's oft-repeated story of his birth. Whenever he lagged behind in studies, mostly concentrating on extra-curricular activities and community initiatives, his mother used to tell him that he was God's special child and that he had better mend his ways and concentrate on studies. For conservative parents, only higher education would make one stand tall in society! Naturally, the mother insisted that her son take studies seriously. Solomon was the third child in a middle class family. The two elder children and the fourth one were also boys. There was no girl child in the family. The mother had a lot of difficulties at the time of birth of the two elder boys who were born at their grandfather's place. The distance between his grandparent's place and his parent's place was about 20 km. In order to reach his grandfather's house, one had to undertake a 20-km bus journey, followed by a bullock cart ride or a long walk.

It was customary then, as it is even now, that women should go to their parents' home for confinement. After the birth of the child, she would stay there for one or two months and then return to her husband's home. But now this practice is slowly disappearing. In most cases, the women now stay at their husband's home and then have the confinement at the hospital. One of the reasons why the health of the new mothers is affected after delivery is lack of rest and proper postnatal care. Postnatal care of the mothers, mostly in the urban areas is very bad, if not totally absent. Then on medical advice, the mothers resort to bottle-feeding the child. Some view it as a nexus between the medical practitioners and the producers of baby food, displacing the requirement of breast feeding, which is very vital for the immune systems of the babies.

When Solomon was to be born, his maternal grandparents came to take his mother to their own house. However, the night before their departure, his mother's grandfather appeared to her in a dream and gave details of the impending birth and the future of the child. He told her that the child would be born within a few days and that this time it would be an easy delivery. He asked her not to go anywhere as the child was to be born in that very home! He revealed that this child too was a boy and that he was to be named as "the boy". He said he had a vision that this boy would, in his later years, build a church and be instrumental in bringing happiness, peace and prosperity to many homes.

6

Meandering Along

Solomon is a Biblical name. King Solomon was the son of King David and ruled Israel for 40 years. It was he who built the temple for the Lord in the 480th year, after the Israelis came out of bondage in Egypt. The *Bible* records that "God gave Solomon wisdom and very great insight, and a breath of understanding as measureless as the sand on the seashore. Solomon's wisdom was greater than the wisdom of all the men of the East". Many Christian parents want their children to acquire knowledge as that of King Solomon. It is no wonder then that Solomon is a favourite name among many Christian families. Contrary to their expectations, many young boys like Solomon have turned out to be a disappointment. However, there are also instances of those who excelled in many walks of life.

Solomon's mother recounted her dream to everyone and pleaded with her parents, much against their will, to allow her to stay in her own home. In our culture, when a deceased person appears in a dream and utters an oracle regarding a situation, the dream is taken seriously. Since she was a religious lady, the family gave credence to her statement and complied with her wish. Nevertheless, because of his present plight after mulling over his mother's dream, Solomon thought that it was a cooked up story. If it were at all true, he would have been in school pursuing studies and not idling on the streets! He felt that owing to his mother's folly, he had landed in his present situation. Perhaps, God had willed it that one day he would be a source of sorrow and trouble to his parents. His mother's painless delivery at the time of his birth, he thought, was an ill omen!

Solomon was at times tormented by this thought of his mother's revelation to him. Till this point in time he had been a very good boy at home, in school and at church. He had all the characteristics of a decent, well-mannered son to his parents. Though he was weak in certain subjects, he always compensated for them with good performance in one or two other subjects and also in extracurricular activities. He always displayed a tendency to be with the weak boys in school and encouraged many to come to the ground and play. He helped many of his friends to perform well in mathematics. In class, everyone used to admire his skill with numbers. But now, he was no longer the role model that he could have been. He thought about his family, friends and all the comforts of life at home, and his present contrary status. He further worried that even if he were not to build a church, that would not be an issue, but if his present way of life should become a cause for destroying the church, that would definitely be a major issue!

The boy, who bore the name of the richest and wisest king in the world, was now a poor and confused 13-year old in the city of Trivandrum! He had to struggle the whole day to earn a meagre sum of 25 paise to get a decent meal, let alone possess a pair of decent clothes and a secure home. For many days, he had to sleep on the platform without a roof over his head. Whenever it rained, he faced a lot of difficulties to find shelter. Since the area was fully occupied by the regulars, others like him were left out. Living was becoming exceedingly tough for him.

The story of the homeless is always melodramatic for the causal observer. In a makeshift tent, the poor man curls up for safety. Many families use all kinds of discarded materials to erect a makeshift home. They use public places for all activities of daily living. In spite of all these experiences of poverty, deprivation, ill-treatment by the elders on the street, and the knowledge of being well-off, Solomon was not convinced to return to his family. He was very adamant in his decision. Though earning and living had become torturous, it was a mystery why he chose to remain on the streets. One day, while he was carrying the luggage of a traveller, he suddenly saw his uncle, who worked as a bus driver, at the bus stand. Instantly, he started to sweat profusely and could almost visualize his uncle taking him to his village, where he would be reprimanded by his family for his act. But fortunately or unfortunately, his uncle stood at a reasonable distance and hence he did not notice Solomon. Attempting to escape that traumatic encounter, he immediately excused himself from the traveller and left the scene. The traveller stood bewildered by the boy's behaviour, but was relieved that he did not run away with his baggage.

All over the world, there are people, young and old, who stray away from their homes due to various socio-economic factors. The interesting 'pull effect' of the street is strange. It offers freedom to be engaged in all kinds of activities, some harmless and some criminal. Moral values are unimportant to wanderers. Probably, this is the reason why it is considered the best and enjoyable option by many runaway boys till they are caught and penalized by the law-enforcing agencies. The delinquent children are then sent to juvenile homes. Many a time, when street children are caught for small acts of misdemeanour, they are set free after a warning by the lenient police. This, in the long run, perpetuates the deviant behaviour in the young offenders.

Boys, who take to begging for their livelihood, are good in doing odd jobs but when they mingle with the grown ups on the streets, especially at nights when they rest in the railway station or beneath the road bridges, they are either forced to become involved in some immoral activities or watch the others engage in such acts quietly. The new entrants are vulnerable to these influences of anti-social elements. For a few, the abuses scar their lives for life. However, at the time when they are abused, they do not question or rebel against the perpetrators of delinquent acts because for some reason or the other, these runaway children have made up their minds not to rejoin their families. Whatever humiliation they encounter, they ignore the gravity and the hurt of it all and live with it for the sake of their freedom, for many a time the situation at home is no different where they would have to contend with an alcoholic, abusive father and the same struggle to survive.

A recent survey in three metropolitan cities of Chennai, Mumbai and Delhi indicates that the majority of streets are full of runaways. A few were those who came to the city because of economic circumstances in the rural areas. Out of the 750 children falling in the age group of 6 to 18, the survey team found that 89 were girls. Some of the girls had earlier worked as servants in big homes and left without telling either the parents or the house-owners. A few were let free by their parents themselves who had spent their entire life on the streets. A sizeable number of children were in that last category. Those who had attended school did not want to resume their studies for different reasons. A few felt the school curriculum was too much and there was no one to help them with their studies at home. In the process, they were intimidated by teachers and fellow students for their below-average performances. They were thus forced to decide to leave their schools and homes as well. A lot of the runaways felt that the time spent in school would affect their earning. They did not realize that their decision would confine them to a strata from which it would be impossible to emerge.

According to the study, a few runaway boys had stolen money from their parents and come to cities in search of opportunities to lead a better life. Many of these runaways live in the hope of making it to the silver screen like their favourite actors. In other fields, it is true that in the 50s, those who had come to cites from poor backgrounds joined various kinds of clubs, like the famous Boys Club of Madras and made it to the top. However, Lady Luck may not bestow her kindness upon all. One reads almost everyday about young boys and girls who leave their homes hoping to become superstars, but eventually land up in jails or end up being employed in the flesh trade. The study also reported that a few girls, mostly in the age group of around 15, also ventured into the city to become a film star. In the majority of such cases, they were encountered by pimps, for whom such naïve girls are easy targets, and enlisted as commercial sex workers. Some were lured by offers of lucrative acting careers in big cities and sold to big dealers who operate flesh trade networks in various metros. The lucky few who escaped from the pimps were forced to become maidservants or pavement hawkers. There were instances of abuse by the police also. Many women's groups have taken up the cause of such women. However, these efforts, though laudable, have resulted in highlighting the data on the existence of the trade rather than helping the victims of abuse. Human trafficking is one of most serious problems in the world today. More than half of the 2.5 million persons trafficked around the world are from Asia. Nearly a third of those, both women and children, are reportedly trafficked every year from Southeast Asia. One unofficial estimate says that in India, every year on an average, about 80,000 girls or women are new entrants into the flesh trade. As tourism increases in the country, another menace has raised its head—that of paedophilia. The danger of children being lured into unspeakable situations has increased immensely.

It is no wonder then that on busy streets and especially at the railway stations and at bus stands in big cities, one can see all kinds of people from different backgrounds and with varied interests. Other than the lucky few who managed to climb up the ladder of success and bid their adieus to the street, there are many more for whom the wayside misery is now the only thing they can identify as their own.

Solomon had now adjusted to his street life completely. He decided to live on the street without thinking of any greater purpose or God's plan for him. Thoughts of his family and house were pushed back in his mind. He grasped whatever work he could lay his hands on. Mostly, he worked as a porter. When there was no work and no money, he starved and lived on tap water. Moreover, he had also learnt the tactics of street life. Whenever he failed to get any job, he would weave out cock and bull stories about his past to stir the sympathy of people. His lies varied from him being orphaned by his parents' death in a fire accident, his tragedy of living with his devil-personified brother, who would beat him severely, and his not-so-caring sister-in-law, and so on. Sometimes he told a story that he was beaten by his uncle for no fault of his and that he had escaped from all of them to eke out his living. The ultimate objective at the end of the day for him was to somehow get one full meal. There were few occasions when he earned extra money. But then, earning 25 paise—whether from his hard work or from all the lies he mouthed—was all that he needed and this kept him contented.

After spending six weeks in Trivandrum, one day Solomon remembered that one of his uncles used to work in Quilon, a big town in Kerala, almost 120 kms away from Trivandrum. After serving in a hospital for about 10 years, his uncle had returned to his native place. Solomon thought that if he could make it to Quilon, he could probably approach the hospital where his uncle worked. Thus, one morning, armed with high hopes and absolutely no money to buy a ticket, he set out on a train journey to reach the town. This was not the first time he was travelling without a ticket. Earlier on, he had gone to other nearby cities only for fun. It was quite common for beggars, street children and hawkers to travel without any ticket. The railways were a boon to many people in those days, when the authorities were not so vigilant.

After spending two days at small intermediate stations, Solomon reached Quilon. It is an old seaport on the Arabian coast and stands on the Ashtamudi Lake. The famous backwaters of Kerala also fall close to this place. Once a city of palaces, Quilon has been known to the outside world, by the time-honoured proverb: "Once you have seen Quilon, you would no more need your *illam* (home)". No wonder, Solomon, who was away from his *illam,* had reached Quilon to make a living. Although he had heard about the famous backwaters with their plush greens and unique species of aquatic life, but he was here to ensure his survival, rather than spending time on pleasure-seeking adventure. He found himself to be a penniless boy in the town who had not taken proper food for the last few days.

Driven to the brink of desperation by hunger, Solomon decided to go to a nearby restaurant to ask for food. He gathered all his courage and asked the person seated behind the counter for some food. Taking advantage of the situation, the hotel owner asked the boy to spread all the raw firewood on the roadside, dry it, bundle and keep it back in the appropriate place. Solomon readily agreed and after completing the work, he was given food for wages. This first contact in the town was a blessing for him. He thought that whenever he was in need of food, he could approach any hotel for this kind of assignment. In the evening, he made the station his dwelling as usual. The earlier occupants of the platform accommodated him without any hard feelings. By now, he had improved his vocabulary in Malayalam and also learnt to present more convincing stories with proper modulation in his voice and body language. Other than his oft-repeated 'orphan story', there were certain occasions when he cooked up other heart-wrenching stories which were bound to work the charm, earning him 5–10 paise depending upon status and sympathy of the benefactor. Generally, most people did not pay much attention to him, and those who did, they just ignored him after a few probing questions.

7

Reminiscing the Past

Solomon's decision of going to the hospital and getting a job there soon escaped his mind. He was not sure in which hospital his uncle had worked. Also, he feared that he would get caught by his family if he gave his uncle's reference. Hence, he completely dismissed the idea of working in the hospital. All his hopes of getting a 'decent' job in the town were completely dashed.

Often we start a journey with great enthusiasm, but once we reach the destination, we wonder why we undertook that journey at all. Many ambitious projects look promising in the beginning, but as time progresses, people realize that these projects will not materialize and hence abandon them. Solomon too was pondering over the ambiguity of it all.

Since he had thwarted the idea of finding recruitment in the hospital, Solomon returned to doing menial jobs. After all, he had to feed himself. He now had to put in more time and efforts than before without earning any better. He felt very frustrated many a time that he had journeyed so far only to do what he was doing in Trivandrum. There was not much difference between the cities. The streets were crowded, and the air was clammy here too. If there was any difference, it was lost on him. He was more concerned about feeding himself than exploring Quilon. Even in this daily struggle, his love for the cinema had not dulled. He would be among the first ones to watch a movie on its release and very proudly narrate the story to other boys of his age whom he had befriended. The boys would often advise him to go back home and not waste his time like a street urchin.

After three months on the street, Solomon did see the logic in going back home but the fear of a thrashing by his parents held him back. He would often wake up from his sleep in the midst of night, trembling with fear and at the same time feeling homesick. He would imagine his parents, uncles and aunts, and even older siblings exercising their authority on him and would wonder till the break of dawn if the elders rightfully exercised their right to discipline the tender hearts. Unlike children of his age, Solomon spent hours thinking about the physical and psychological punishments that harmed the growth and development of a child.

Unfortunately, for most adults, punishment is the only tool of discipline they know. Very few understand the complex matrix of power, relation, violence, and abuse that underlies punishment as they normally perceive.

Solomon recollected the occasions in the past when his parents scolded him even for minor faults. Once he had gone to visit a big festival at a nearby village with one of his friends. He went there directly from school and returned late in the night, some time around 9 pm. By the time he reached home, there was a big commotion in his house. The whole family was worried because of his prolonged absence. As soon as he step foot in his house, he was beaten squarely on his buttocks with a broom stick by his father.

Compared to that, such prolonged absence from his home spelt 'doomsday' for him. He thought that if he returned home now, it would end his life, literally! He loved his life dearly to let it end miserably at the hands of his parents and brothers. He strongly believed that every child was eligible to four basic rights—right to survival, right to protection, right to development, and right to participation.

In the present context, it behoves us to reflect on the fact that God Almighty has a purpose for which we are called upon to live here on this earth. Unaware of it, we tend to fret and fume over our circumstances when we fail to fulfil

His purposes. He knows us, our strengths and weaknesses. He, in His wisdom, may allow us to go through adversities and sufferings. By this, He builds in us an immunity to hardship and also gives us the strength to deal with adversity. As Job says, "God knows the way that He takes; when He has tested me I will come forth as gold." The Creator will do with us what He chooses to. He moulds us according to what is in store for us. "Go down to the potter's house, and there I will give you my message", says the Lord. "Like clay in the hand of the potter, so are you in my hand." When the time comes, God will lift His chosen people—families, communities and nations—even from the pit of destruction. Therefore, we must learn to do the things that are right to the best of our ability and leave the rest to God. He will provide us with the things according to what He has planned at the appropriate time.

Back in school, Solomon had harboured the desire to become a great officer after completing his studies. He had dreamt, with his very being, of becoming a great development economist or a district collector or even a philanthropist so that he could help others, especially the vulnerable and the underprivileged. But now that long-cherished dream had vanished into thin air. If he were to continue like this, he would lose the literary skills he had obtained at school, let alone becoming an instrument of change for the betterment of others! But he was not bothered about all these things. In his heart of hearts, he was under the impression that God's invisible hands would one day lift him from the ditch into which he had fallen.

Once in school, students were asked to give a speech on the political situation of the district, which was fraught with conflict between the Indian National Congress Party and the district Congress leaders over the selection of a candidate for the MLA seat. The entire district was against the INCP and had put up a rebel candidate. The rebel candidate won the MLA seat. It was Solomon's father who had played an instrumental role in organizing the campaign for the rebel candidate. At the speech competition, Solomon's analysis of the situation was acclaimed by all and his class teacher had pronounced that he will "become a great politician or an administrator one day".

Street boys are always on the lookout for jobs to keep them going. For them, the day ahead is more important than their families. No wonder, Solomon too had forced the thoughts of his family into oblivion. Similarly, all thoughts of going back to school were now a forgotten agenda. He had just completed three months on the streets. He knew that his school would have reopened and all his friends would be wondering what happened to him. He also knew that since he had not written the eighth standard examination, the possibility of him joining the ninth standard was nil. If at all he wanted to pursue studies, he had to sit in the same class again, with his juniors, while his friends would be in the ninth standard. What a shame! What a pity it would be for him, who was acknowledged to be a good performer in extracurricular activities. His peers loved him for his friendly behaviour. He felt ashamed by the thought that his friends would be in a higher class, and he realized that he would not be able to withstand the humiliation.

Every time a Sunday dawned, Solomon's thoughts would invariably return to his family. Generally, Sunday was the day when all the family members went to church together. They would dress up neatly to participate in the church services. They also enjoyed good meals which included non-vegetarian delicacies and desserts. In the evening, they were served snacks along with tea. On some rare Sundays, they all went to the beach or visited friends and relatives and at times went for a movie. Now that he was living on the streets away from all these delights, he understood the importance of small gestures such as eating together. A smile would often break on his face whenever his thoughts took him back to his village and the squabbles he had at his home. Normally, these were dinner-time arguments which would last till late in the evening. The following morning, they would forget everything and come together to attend to their daily chores. Home is a place of tranquillity and peace. At his home, sharing and caring were demonstrated and forgiveness was imbibed into the minds of everyone, young and old.

While he missed all his family members immensely, he had no idea as to how much his parents missed him.

Naturally, they would have missed their son, far more than he could imagine. No one could have substituted him in the family. As a matter of fact, his parents had forgotten all his misdeeds. They had spent a lot of their money and time in trying to search him. Not a day passed when his parents did not pray to God for his safe return. The irony was that Solomon and his parents viewed the situation in totally different ways. While he thought that he had sinned against his family and that he would never be forgiven, the scene at his home was different. While he thought it was an unpardonable sin, his parents were completely non-judgmental about it. They were eager to have him come home and resume his studies at school.

8

Finding a Ray of Hope

Solomon's parents were gradually getting more anxious about the welfare of their son as each day passed. They spent much of their money on advertisements in local newspapers. Since absolutely no contact could be established with their lost son, they could only imagine what might have happened. Solomon's disappearance had struck his family, especially his father, like a bolt from the blue. His father had started growing a beard in his agony. He could not handle the thought of the suffering and pain of his son, living alone somewhere out of his view and reach.

At times, he even imagined that something untoward may have happened to him. The poor father was in great mental distress, pining for the return of the 'prodigal'. However, his friends prevailed upon him not to lose hope of the boy's homecoming.

Solomon's mother was also greatly distressed thinking of her missing son. Not a moment passed when she would not pray for her son to return. She now started each day by visiting temples, talking to the preachers and asking them to pray for her son's safe return. Her eyes invariably darted towards the door of the house; anxious eyes searching for a mere glimpse of her beloved son. So much so, at times, she even kept the front door unlocked in the hope that if her Solomon returns in the dead of the night, they should not lose even a split second in searching for the key and unlocking the door.

Apart from his parents, Solomon's siblings too started feeling his absence as time rolled on. They missed his heroics on special family occasions, the pranks that they played on each other away from the vigilance of their parents. Though all the brothers bickered often, they also had a special bonding and love which was not always expressed in so many words, but a slap on the back or a friendly punch on the shoulder conveyed more than words could.

The family's gloom increased manifold when Solomon's birthday came. There was an eerie silence in the house, which in better days used to reverberate with booming laughter, constant chattering and bliss. Each year, Solomon's birthday was marked as a special occasion when he would receive gifts and accolades from his loved ones. His mother would make his favourite fish curry and a sweet dish made of coconut and jaggery. The day would begin with an early morning bath and then a visit to the church to seek blessings of God and to listen to the friendly admonishes of the parish priest, who would waggle his finger at Solomon while he spoke. But this year, there was no familiar smell of fish curry wafting in the air or the sound of coconuts being grated in the old-fashioned grinding stone.

His mother did visit the church and as she knelt down in prayer at one of the pews, tears started streaming down her face. She used to put on a brave face and carry on her days because she did not want her other children to get affected by her sorrow. But here, in the presence of her Maker, she could give in to her emotions. She asked God that if her son was a special boy, who was to be of service to Him just like the Biblical Samuel, as told to her in her dream, why was he taken away from her? She prayed for some sign so that she would know he was safe and if indeed he was serving the church in some manner. The priest offered her some consolation and asked her to keep the faith and told her that her son would not be abandoned and reminded her of the verse in Psalm 91 which speaks of God's protection. Solomon's mother returned from church with renewed hope. However, she could not bring herself to cook fish curry on this day, although it was a favourite with the other children too.

The family had bought a piece of land in the town with the intention of building a home. But because of Solomon's unexpected departure, the idea had to be dropped for the time being. As of now, their main concern was to wait for his return. Such was the yearning on the part of the parents to receive him and accept him back into their fold. Solomon's parents had witnessed a few families in the neighbourhood who have had a runaway ward. The parents' love and affection had drawn these children back home. They believed that their son too would one day return as they had no doubt that Solomon knew how much they loved him. But no such intuition worked in Solomon's mind. Adults are often on the horns of dilemma because of their ego, not realizing that conflicting thoughts can be resolved by submitting to God's will. In case of Solomon, it was less the case of ego, which afflicts adults more than children. It was the fear of the reception he thought he would receive and the shame of repeating a year in the same class which kept him away.

One day, during a casual conversation with one of his street companions, Solomon told him about the matchbox-making factory owned by his grandfather in his native village. Solomon recounted how every time he visited his grandfather, he made it a point to visit the matchbox unit, where he tried to help by doing odd jobs like arranging the matchsticks in a wooden frame, helping the technician to dip the block of matchsticks in a frame containing hot liquid wax and then again in a pool of chemical plate. Thereafter, he used to place a stipulated number of matchsticks in small boxes, some containing 40 sticks while others 60. Although he was not fully trained in any specific task in that unit, he was aware of all the activities and also enjoyed helping the people working there. After listening to his narration with rapt attention, his companions advised him to go to Punalur in Kerala or Sivakasi in Tamil Nadu to get a permanent employment.

The idea sounded good to Solomon, and he decided to go to Sivakasi, more so since it was situated in Tamil Nadu. There would be no language barrier for him. He, who lived an aimless life, could finally see light at the end of the tunnel and a probable release from his long sufferings, should he be placed in a job, or so he thought. Solomon had not been long in Quilon to form any friendships as such. He longed for companionship just like any other human being. He was grateful for the useful suggestion and thanked the other boy for giving him vital tips.

Yet again, he was confronted with the question as to how he would reach Sivakasi? In those days, the concept of child labour was not so widely acknowledged. The match and fire-cracker industry employed a large number of children till recently. It was the result of a sustained campaign against fire-crackers, as they are pollutants and are made by using child labour, that brought the focus on Sivakasi and the children working there. However, it has not ended child labour. In those days, factory owners would employ children as they would have to pay them only a fraction of the wages for the same working hours or even longer than an adult worker. The owners knew that the children would not be in a position to protest because it meant instant firing from the job. Most owners would provide a simple meal for the child workers, which, for the majority of the children, was the only substantial meal of the day. For the parents of the children, it was a logical arrangement; at least, the child was earning his keep instead of wasting his time in useless pursuits and was getting a meal too in the bargain! Exploitation indeed has myriad forms.

Sivakasi is situated in the dry belt area of Virudhunagar district. The livelihood of the people is ensured partly by agriculture and partly by the match industry. Sivakasi was and still is considered notorious for employing children in the match industry. It has production units for matches, fireworks and also a printing industry and together these employ more than 50 per cent of child labour, both boys and girls. Many of these matches or firework factories are run by unlicensed sub-contractors. However, the city has had an honour of being called 'mini Japan' by Pt Jawaharlal Nehru, the country's first Prime Minister. The growth of these industries, along with other allied industries, not only increased the income of the people, but also of the state and central governments.

The distance to Sivakasi from Quilon was about 160 kms. And Solomon, as always, had no savings. He resorted to the best and the only way known to him; he would travel without a ticket. In spite of repeated warnings, and a shove here and a push there, he continued to travel without ticket. Whether this new journey would be a blessing or a curse, he did not know. But he was determined to work harder. He realized that it was at least worth the risk. He took leave of his friends and promised them that one day he would come back to visit them all, although in his heart of hearts he knew he would not see them again. He took the night passenger train from Quilon station and boarded the third class unreserved compartment—something that is not seen today. The coach was too crowded to provide any comfort, but he had long learnt not to complain. He made himself comfortable in a corner of a berth and went off to sleep.

In the 60s, most of the trains had only three types of compartments—the first class, the second class and the third class. Some of the compartments were unreserved. Today, we see different types of compartments with varied levels of comfort including sleeping berths. The so-called third class is completely abolished now. Over the years, the mode of travel and trains have improved. In fact, one can measure a country's growth with the progress of its public as well as the private transport services, as they clearly mirror the progress the country has made. It was strange but true that until the 80s even to buy a bike or a scooter one had to make a booking with advance payment and wait for months together. These days one can easily walk into any showroom and purchase his preferred vehicle across the counter. The country has come a long way from bullock cart and horse driven-transport system to air travel of different kinds.

Realizing that the train's rumbling had stopped and so had its motion, Solomon groggily opened his eyes and looked around to see only a few passengers left in the compartment. He stepped out onto the platform thinking that he had reached his destination. He noticed that there was hardly anyone on the platform but thought no more of it as the clock on the platform showed that it was 4 am. He thought that at a devilish time like this, even a crowded city like Sivakasi's railway station was bound to be empty. Without giving it much thought, he prepared himself for a better life full of opportunities. Little did he know that only in a few minutes from now, he would get a stinging slap on his face.

Seeing the boy coming out from the compartment at an odd hour, a policeman on duty came up to him to interrogate. From experience, the policeman understood that the boy was a vagabond, travelling without a ticket. Though the best course of action would have been to allow him to get out of the station with a warning, being the custodian of law and a bully, the policeman wanted to flaunt his authority. On being asked by the policeman, Solomon had to accept that he had got into the train from Quilon and that he had no ticket. The policeman slapped Solomon across the face, leaving his ears ringing.

It was the beginning of the hard journey Solomon had embarked upon. It took him a while to accept that hundreds of young boys and girls were given similar treatment day in and day out for their 'misbehaviour'. He wondered why the society deemed it necessary to bestow corporal punishment upon children to discipline them. Do children deserve punitive action for the mistakes they commit? Or should they be left alone? Should they not be counselled and helped to change their behaviour? The thoughts kept crisscrossing his mind as he rubbed his cheek which was stinging and the fingers of the policeman showed up as red welts across his face.

The *Bible* says, "Spare the rod and spoil the child." Some use this verse to justify corporal punishment. There is another saying also; if one does not get disciplined at the age of five, he would then never be disciplined, even at the age of 50. In the 60s and 70s, in spite of children being treated severely, the incidence of child abuse was low. Today, on the contrary, cases of child abuse—physical, psychological and social—are widely prevalent all over the world. The truth is that some families have not learnt the art of child rearing, though there are many educated families who meticulously rear pets in their homes and do not have time for their children. It is sad that a few, holding high positions, are obsessed with their career development and income-earning prospects, and neglect their children. Parents have a great responsibility in taking care of the children who are indeed God's gift to families.

This was the first time that Solomon was slapped on his face. He had had his share of beatings earlier too but never had he been hit on his face. He was immediately thrown out of the railway station. Wiping the stream of tears from his face, he looked around and noticed that he had reached a place called Senkottai, 95 kms from Quilon, half the distance from his scheduled destination. Senkottai is situated on the foot hills of the Western Ghats, and is the nearest railway station to Courtallam. Solomon still had a long way to go.

Before state re-organization, Senkottai was part of Travancore Samasthanam. In 1956, after the State Re-organization Act was passed, the Tamil-speaking area of Kerala (the present Kanyakumari district) and the Senkottai Taluk of Quilon district were added to Tamil Nadu state.

Solomon remembered reading something about Courtallam in his geography book. He had read that the place is adorned with breathtaking views of waterfalls, making it a popular tourist spot. No wonder hordes of people visited these falls throughout the year, he thought. It is believed that an oil bath taken in the Courtallam waterfalls rejuvenates the body and mind, as the rain water flowing through the hills carries with it medicinal extracts from the lush herbal plants on the way. Many have claimed that a bath in these waters have a soothing effect, it help the old to feel rejuvenated and the sick to heal rapidly. But the cool atmosphere and weather did not impact Solomon's mind, may be because he was neither old nor sick at that point of time.

9
New Friendship

It was about five in the morning when Solomon stepped out of the small railway station. Not knowing what to do, he again dozed off to sleep on the floor of the front hall of the station. When he got up, he found the station buzzing with activity, though not on the same scale as the other stations he had lived in.

The usual question that arose in his mind was where and how was he to get his next meal. The excitement which he had felt when travelling to Sivakasi had ebbed by now. He no longer felt adventurous as he had when dodging the ticket inspector. All he felt now was a hollow feeling in the pit of his stomach which clamoured for nourishment. He really did not dwell over his transformation from a cosseted boy to a runaway, a street-child and a ticket less traveller. Then all of a sudden, he noticed a boy who was about four or five years older than himself, looking at him intently. He signalled Solomon to come closer. He was better-dressed as compared to Solomon. The two started talking as though they had known each other since long and friendship blossomed between them. Solomon had just been looking for some affectionate concern from someone to erase the wound the policeman had inflicted, and here came that healing touch from unexpected quarters.

Both the boys shared details about their backgrounds and realized that they were comfortable in the company of each other. After all, both chose to make the street their home for very trivial reasons. They both had left their respective homes without telling anyone, unmindful of the consequences and uncertain about their future. At the end of the conversation, a deal was struck between the two. This was the first time in his life that Solomon had entered into a negotiation. The elder boy, Lokesh, had too left his family. He claimed to be a good singer, but had a physical disability: he was born with one normal hand while the other hand was half the normal length. He could be classified as being differently-abled. He wanted to reach Madras so that he could sing in films. His aim was to become a great singer. The younger boy's aim, however, was to get a job, preferably in the match industry. One had a long-term vision of making it to a position of greatness, and the other had a short-term vision of just getting a job to meet day-to-day needs. The partnership was to ensure food security to one and fame in life to the other. One was looking for a little ink dot penned in a corner of the picture and the other was visualizing a large canvas with colourful strokes.

They were different from each other in many ways, yet they both complemented each other.

Lokesh, having just arrived on the street from an area in Kerala with some money in his pocket, wanted someone's support to take his move forward and guide him, first to reach Madras and then to further help him make his way to a film studio. The idea fascinated Solomon greatly as he was a fan of matinee idol MG Ramachandran, popularly known as MGR, and also because he himself took great interest in acting, having enacted certain roles in his school functions.

As soon as Lokesh mentioned a 'film studio', Solomon's train of thoughts went back to the time he enacted the role of Kattabomman, a native rebel against the British rule, for his school annual day function. The legend of Kattabomman was the subject of a couple of films too, which were made in the regional language. Solomon was selected for the role because of his skill in dialogue delivery. As was expected of him by teachers as well as students, he played the role extremely well. The story was about a courageous Indian in Tamil Nadu who stood against the rule of the British, mobilized the public against foreigners and fought for the independence of the country. As a result, he was sent to the gallows by the British. His excellent execution of the role won him accolades from his headmaster, his class teacher and all the students. No wonder then that the idea of going to Madras and being at a cinema studio was more attractive than becoming an ordinary wage earner in a matchbox industry at Sivakasi. He started dreaming of becoming a great actor and his friend a renowned singer.

Very often, life pushes one between the dichotomy of pursuing a definite plan involving a lot of hard work and promise of a slow, sustained growth and a quick fanciful achievement of a position which ensures frills of glamour, opulence and popularity. The second appears to be more appealing and compelling than the first in most cases. In such situations, one does not weigh the pros and cons and tends to let the heart rule rather than the head.

Both the boys could not think beyond their dreams. They were in their own dreamland where they continued to tend their fancy plans. Someone has rightly said that concrete and realistic action is imperative to realize dreams. It is true that if one does not have a dream, one would be lost in this world. Dreamers always are the trend-setters. They both felt that if they teamed up, they could achieve their respective goals. Hence, their minds resolved on working to achieve their goals. As far as Solomon was concerned, for the immediate moment, all he needed was some money and regular food. If someone could assure him those things, he had no problem in going anywhere. He also wanted new clothes. The older boy had brought a lot of money from his home. Would he have pilfered it from his parents' savings, the boy wondered.

Solomon was happy that he had a new friend on whom he could depend and who had an aim in life. He considered Lokesh as a messiah sent by God to take care of him. He, in his young mind, concluded that if everyone took five minutes each day to go out of their way to make someone else's life a little happier, the world would be a better place to live in. His Sunday school teacher had always advised the students never to miss an opportunity to help others. Solomon further thought that this friendship agreement was worth pursuing. They both were eagerly waiting for the shops to open their shutters so that they could buy new clothes for Solomon. In the meantime, they washed themselves at the station and had their first breakfast together at a small eatery outside the station. It was after many weeks that Solomon had a good breakfast, which was not earned, but God-given. He felt at home. Whatever thoughts of going back home had managed to make some space in his mind were again pushed back because of this chance-meeting with Lokesh. The steam from the pristine white *idlis*, nestling on the green bed of the banana leaf and the aroma of piping hot *sambar* made him hungrier. Solomon did not mind that the *sambar* scalded his tongue when he fell upon the *idlis*. When the waiter, another boy who was not much older than the two boys themselves, asked if there was anything else they wanted, Solomon vigorously nodded his head and managed to order some *vadas*, a favourite of his, although his mouth was full. Finally, replete with the food and the fragrant coffee that followed the meal, both the boys stepped out in the hot sun. They wandered around a bit, waiting for the shops to open.

In those days, life was more slow-paced. It was not like the present times when everyone seems to be rushing off somewhere although the destination appears unclear. Shops in the main market opened when the day was well underway. Lokesh and Solomon sat on a cement culvert by the road and watched as the shutters of the shops were rolled up one by one. They saw the shops being swept out, after which the owner would quickly begin his incantations addressed to his favourite deity who adorned a corner of his shop, praying for good business that day. Lokesh and Solomon stepped into a shop when they saw the shop-keeper finally turn away from the pictures of various gods and goddesses on the wall. The shop smelt fragrant with the wisps of sandalwood incense curling up around the pictures. Both boys spent some very enjoyable time looking over various clothes that were on display. Solomon had grown taller in the past months. He had out-grown his shorts that he had left home with. He felt he needed to buy trousers as he was working now, almost a grown-up, and was no longer a school boy. He delighted in selecting shirts and trousers, holding them up against himself while he looked at himself in the mirror. He had not done this for a long time. He remembered going to the market with his mother for shopping before Christmas when clothes and other gifts were bought for everyone. He remembered the little squabbles he used to have with his brothers over the toys or the number of rose cookies, which are a speciality made during Christmas, the other had and his eyes misted over. Lokesh slapped him on the back in commiseration and Solomon shook himself out of the memory. They finally selected a shirt, in a pattern popularly known as 'Madras check' and a pair of khaki-coloured trousers to go with it. Solomon had, by now, become more practical about certain things. It was no longer a situation where he need not have bothered whether clothes were laundered or not. He thought the khaki colour would not show dirt so easily as others.

Lokesh paid for the clothes that Solomon had selected while the latter watched admiringly how the former quickly counted the notes just like he had seen his father do. Solomon accepted the gifts, the first in many months, gratefully. They came out of the shop, clutching the paper packet carefully and headed towards the bus stand. They decided to board the first bus to Madras as if they already had an appointment at a studio. The next short journey they took together was a happy walk to the bus stand.

When they reached the bus stand, they found that there was no bus for Madras till midnight. Since they had ample time to kill, they decided to walk towards Madras so that by evening they could not only have seen the countryside, but would also have covered, probably, about half the distance to Madras. A journey well-begun is a good sign of reaching the destination on time. However, only when we embark upon the arduous road do we notice the hurdles and road blocks. One has to be prepared to meet them with determination to reach the goal envisioned in the action plan.

It was June. The weather was pleasant, if not salubrious. It was the monsoon season and the sky was grey with clouds. Although it was humid, the constant breeze from the adjacent Western Ghats cooled them, making walking a less tiring affair. As the journey progressed, they talked about their families, friends, their ambitions and how they were fortunate to have had the pleasure of each one's company. Occasionally, they rested on the side of the road under trees, stopping once in a while for some tea. When they felt hungry, they stopped at the wayside snack vendors for some snacks made of the typical red-plantain commonly grown in Kerala and Tamil Nadu. It was fascinating for the boys to see the vendor expertly slice the plantain lengthwise and dip it in a batter and slide it into the hot oil. They watched the fritters bubble in the hot oil as the aroma wafted in the air. The fritters were ladled out of the oil and handed over in a leaf plate after some seasoning was sprinkled on them.

As they munched on the banana fritters, they passed through some villages and came across some coconut groves. They saw some men shimming up the trees with the agility of acrobats and disappear at the top of the trees amidst the palm fronds. The boys looked longingly at the pile of green coconuts lying on the ground as they were thirsty. One of the men looked at them and asked, "Where are you from?" They told him they had come from Quilon and were on their way to Madras. The man seemed impressed. He then asked if they wanted some coconut water. The boys nodded eagerly. The man selected two coconuts and quickly sliced off the top of the nuts with his sharp knife and gave them to the boys. They took the coconuts and drank the sweet water gratefully.

When they finished the water, they handed over the empty shells to the man who halved them and scooped out the tender white translucent flesh from the centre. The boys ate the sweet-tasting coconut while answering the questions put to them by the man rather guardedly. They thanked the man when they finished and again set off towards Madras, their El Dorado. As they neared another village, they saw paddy fields interspersed with empty land along both sides of the road. There were big square-shaped irrigation wells where people were bathing. Each well was about 10 to 15 feet deep with steps leading into the well. There were youngsters diving and swimming in them and enjoying themselves.

This was the first time Solomon had seen a square-shaped well. In his native place, he always took a bath in the shallow river. The wells in his native district were mainly used to supply drinking water. However, he bathed in river water or irrigation canals or tanks only when he went to his grandfather's village. Solomon could not resist appreciating the scenic surroundings that were partly dry and partly green, with big irrigation wells providing water to the paddy fields. This beautiful little haven reminded him of his grandfather's village Ethavillai.

Ethavillai had a beautiful river passing through its paddy fields. Since the river was perennial, its water was available throughout the year for irrigation. The farmers therefore used to grow crops twice a year. Along with the paddy fields, beautiful banana fields also formed a part of the landscape. The paddy fields were fenced with coconut and arecanut trees. Also, there were plenty of mango gardens which promised excellent fruits and lovely shade to play under in the summer heat. Solomon was reminded of all the bananas, mangoes and cashew nuts that he had so liberally pluck from the trees and gorged on greedily.

The lovely spot which Solomon and Lokesh had discovered was a bewitching indeed with all its natural glories. Apart from the wells and the ripe fields, there were native flower plants which attracted beautiful butterflies and bees. The drone of the bees and the fluttering butterflies filled the air and was as enticing as a lover's song to his beloved. At a distance, Solomon could also see a vast tract of pasture land with a good number of cattle grazing lazily on the lush green grass. The sun was out and shining brightly over the fields. The mesmerizing scene was very inviting to

Solomon. He wanted to take a dip in the cool waters of the well. But Lokesh did not want to waste any more time in reaching his destination.

Since both the boys were strangers to each other and they differed on opinions, a mild argument ensued between the two. While Lokesh strongly felt that they should not waste their time in unwanted things like sight-seeing and indulging in a little adventure, Solomon wanted to relish each part of the journey. Both the boys had their own view points. Lokesh pointed out that it was unnecessary for Solomon to want to have a dip in the well because he had had a bath. He felt it was a waste of time to watch children play in the water. Solomon tried to reason that it reminded him of his grandfather's place and it was not a waste of time if one were to enjoy one's surroundings. It was not as if they had a fixed appointment to keep, was Solomon's argument. Lokesh countered that Solomon had left his home far behind him so what was the use of remembering what was left behind? When Solomon pleaded that he wanted to spend some time there, Lokesh was not convinced and told him that he would carry on without him and he (Solomon) was free to do whatever he wanted on his own.

Lokesh: "Solomon, let us not bother too much about going to the well and watching the children play. You already had a bath."

Solomon: "*Anna* (elder brother), the scene reminded me of my native place. Please let me spend some time here."

Lokesh: "You already left your native place and have come a long way… Now what is the need to worry about?"

Solomon: "*Anna*, how would a few more minutes matter?"

Lokesh: "Solomon, after some time you will say you want to go back to your home."

Solomon: "It is not like that *Anna*! Please let me spend some time here."

Lokesh: "If that is so, I am going on my way. You do whatever you want."

And thus the friendship, which both had felt was a benediction for them, ended abruptly. Parting ways between friends is always painful. Though their goals were similar, unfortunately, they did not learn the give and take policy. Had they been mature enough, they could have worked together by giving each other the required space. It would have been better if they had consciously made some adjustments to sink their differences. The survival of any relationship and even an institution like family depends wholly upon people giving each other the space they need. It is here the culture of families and communities plays a vital role. A great virtue in Asian cultures is that people are generally patient and resilient, and can strike a compromise during conflicts. But lately, the scenario is changing with focus on individual rights and privileges, thanks to globalization and competitive trade relationships.

10

Goodbye My Angel

As a group, people earnestly and meticulously plan things but while implementing the same, either they get distracted or face temporary difficulties, as a result of which they get disappointed and abandon the plan. On the other hand, diligent and conscientious people always keep their goal, mission and vision in mind and never let adverse circumstances blur their vision, even if short-term benefits appear more attractive. History is replete with examples of such persons who made it to the top because of their perseverance. By the same token, history also records the names of those who lost all their credibility because they yielded to pressure from outside.

The friendship between two hitherto unknown strangers, which started at about six in the morning for the common goal of reaching Madras had since run into rough waters. The deal stood broken because of Solomon's insistence on taking a dip in a well—a petty desire though it was—whereas the more goal-oriented Lokesh wanted to continue the journey. The latter must have felt cheated by Solomon's limited perception of the goal. No doubt it was a breach of trust on Solomon's part, but at the same time, Lokesh could have been a little more understanding and patient. Since both were very new to life's challenges, they had not fully understood the principle of putting others' need before one's own, illustrating the weight self-centredness exercised over that of consideration of another's point of view. But this is not something that afflicts only the young. Adults are equally self-centred, if not more, which has far more serious consequences than the self-centredness of children.

People are always in a hurry to do things and accomplish them. They tend to blame the other key figures and withdraw from the deal, if they fail. People should learn to trust others and their ability to do things differently that may be mutually beneficial. This calls for discernment of individual interests and intentions in a conflict. One should be prepared to subordinate one's own interests to those of the other, if they aspire to achieve their common goals. The same principle applies to the pursuit of national interests also. In this age of interdependence and peaceful coexistence between nation-states, the leadership should strive to understand the genuine needs and intentions of others and constructively execute plans for peace, progress and prosperity of their respective nations.

After Lokesh continued on his journey alone, Solomon took a leisurely bath in the well, and felt clean and fresh, and looked as good as he was when he left his home. He would have probably felt rejuvenated in his body like the Syrian army commander, Nagaman, who was cleansed of his leprosy after dipping himself seven times in the river Jordan.

The *Bible* says that Nagaman's flesh was restored and became clean like that of a young child. In Solomon's case, although he used to wash himself under the public tap, it was not the same as this bath in the irrigation well. His indulgence, which had cost him a friend and benefactor, seemed worthwhile because he felt a kind of peace which he had not felt since the fateful day he boarded the bus to Trivandrum.

Since Lokesh had not been petty and churlish and not taken away the clothes he had bought for Solomon, the old and dirty clothes were immediately discarded and he put on his new ones. Solomon felt completely refreshed, both physically and mentally. He felt the same confidence coming back to him that he had felt when he set out for Trivandrum. After having spent three months in the company of many people and earning his livelihood, he was sure that he had braced himself to face any crisis and live his life with new courage and confidence.

After dressing himself in his new clothes and preening a bit, Solomon felt lonely all over again. He wished Lokesh had been there to see him. Though he had parted ways with Lokesh, he began to miss the company of the boy who was not less than a benefactor to him. He remembered their short but joyous and refreshing friendship. It had been quite some time, almost three months to be precise, since Solomon had made any 'real' friend in the true sense of the word. He had made some friends while he was living in the streets but they were all street urchins who had no other option but to spend their lives on the grimy streets. Lokesh was the one who not only offered him his friendship, but also helped him getting clean clothes and taught him what it meant to have an aim in life. Solomon was sure that Lokesh was a God-sent angel who had come to guide him in his course. But that angel had now parted ways with him. Solomon felt miserable and lonely again. He weakened for a moment, thinking whether his insistence to take that bath was well worth the friendship that it cost him. But he had, by this time, learnt to live with compromises and make little of people leaving him. He egged his determination on and resolved to move ahead, with or without anybody.

Taking small steps towards the road, Solomon's thoughts were not completely removed from Lokesh. The benevolent acts done by his 'angel' had reminded him of a similar episode that was encountered by his grandfather. On one of his visits to his village, his grandfather had told him of how he too had met his own personal 'angel'. Walking alone on a lonely and unfamiliar path in the dead of the night, Solomon's grandfather was greatly perturbed and was groping in the dark to find his way home. But then he saw a middle-aged woman walking ahead of him. On seeing him, she turned back and walked slowly towards him. She engaged him in an interesting conversation on world affairs. When they both reached a crossroad, the woman bade him goodbye and took another path. From then on, the terrain was familiar to his grandfather. He could easily walk home without any anxiety. The lady went on her way and as grandfather watched her, to his surprise, she could not be seen, even while she was within his field of vision. Could she have been an angel sent by God to help his grandfather?

Solomon likened his own experience with that of his grandfather. Many weary travellers in the past have recounted similar strange encounters. Having heard of such experiences, Solomon felt that the Almighty had wrought all the favours to him since that morning. He was rejuvenated and was eager to undertake the journey of his life. He did not regret leaving Quilon, although he was not very sure if the coins that were tinkling in his pocket would last him as far as Madras. Solomon dived into his pockets to feel the money with his hands and was once again reminded of Lokesh, for it was he who had given him that money after buying the new pair of clothes for him. Solomon hoped against hope that he would meet Lokesh on the way and resolved to apologize to him for his selfish and childish attitude and give him an undertaking that hereafter he would not leave him.

Musing over this, Solomon continued to walk and before long reached a bus stop. He boarded a bus from there—thanks to the spare money he had—and reached Kadaiyanallur. After buying some ground nuts to munch on and with nothing else to do in the town, he went as usual looking for a quiet corner to lie down for the night. Tired as he was, he dozed off as soon as he lay down. The next morning, the usual din and clamour of a bus stand woke him up.

Realizing that he was short on money, he began to offer his services to carry the luggage of travellers. This continued for almost a week. Since he had not been able to get any suitable job in this town too, the idea of going to the match industry again seized his mind. Solomon decided to head towards Sivakasi. After all, he could not continue for ever to act like a luggage carrier and survive on the few pennies that were thrown at him. Eventually, he arrived at another town, Sankaranairkoil, commonly called Sankaran Koil, on the way to Sivakasi. When he learnt that this town had a railway station, he was greatly relieved as he always found sleeping at the railway station trouble-free, if not more comfortable compared to a bus stand.

The following day was a hard one. He was totally broke. Worse, he could find no means of earning his bread. He had not had anything except for a handful of ground nuts the previous evening. As usual, with the free-flowing tap water at the railway station, he quenched his thirst and quelled his hunger pangs for a while.

As the morning train arrived, Solomon saw many travellers with heavy luggage. He was sure that we would earn well that day as he could expect better alms for heavy luggage. But no one hired his service. Just as he was about to lose all hope and sleep on an empty stomach at night, he noticed an old man with a boy behind him carrying a tin trunk and a bag with great difficulty and walking towards the exit gate from the other end of the platform. As soon as Solomon saw that the boy was finding it difficult to carry the luggage, he offered to help. The old man looked him over and directed the boy to share a portion of the load. The man appeared to be wealthy and was on a pilgrimage to the temples in the state. He had come to this town to visit a temple which was about two kilometres from the station. On the way, he bought something to eat, and after eating most of it, he offered the remaining to the boys. While both hungrily shared their food, the man asked Solomon about his background. Aware that the old man was listening, he painted a very sad picture of his life. A deal was struck that both the boys would carry the man's load in turns. They would accompany him wherever he went, which was mostly temple towns. Apart from carrying his luggage, they were supposed to provide any kind of domestic help that he needed at their place of stay, and if need be, even massage his body, especially his legs with oil, so that he would be fit enough to walk the next day to another temple town. Although Solomon did not consider this a good job, he was acutely aware of the fact that he had no other means to earn money. Hence he agreed to accompany the old man. As long as the boys were ready to do the job assigned to them there was no problem and in return they could get three square meals. The arrangement seemed decent enough not to be refused.

That day, the sun was burning to its full capacity. Its furious heat roasted everyone, especially the tarred road on which the boys had to walk with a heavy load on their head. Sweat poured profusely from their bodies and the soles their feet were already half-burnt. It had been almost 30 minutes that Solomon was carrying the load on his head. The heat along with the load was making it even more unbearable to walk. As a result, he slowed down and lagged behind as they walked. After a few minutes, he decided to opt out of this service. He longed to rest and take a good nap under the shady trees. Although he needed money and the assured food which the man had promised, he could not continue to labour in such an inhumane manner. The avenues of shady trees on both the sides of the road were too inviting for him to continue with his laborious journey. Though he may be in the worst of situations for a boy of his background, he was still a child nonetheless. He told the old man that he could not continue with the journey and the duo left without asking him anything else. Solomon was left alone again.

He was completely heartbroken by now. Could a purpose-driven life emerge only from a broken heart? The idea of bidding goodbye to this hard and cruel life and going back to his family flashed in his mind again. But he pushed the thought away as soon as it had come. Solomon had firm belief that Almighty God must have a plan for him. God in His wisdom and out of His mercy would certainly lift him up and lead him to the destination that He had proposed for him. He resolved not to look back and continue to search for that much-awaited breakthrough. As he started looking around for a clue to proceed further, he saw a cluster of houses at a distance and walked towards them. He could see a small typical Tamil Nadu village with an assorted, shapeless cluster of mud huts, roofed with thatch and only a narrow path leading to a big street. The street was fairly long and had good houses on both sides; houses which probably belonged to rich merchants or landlords, and were plastered with lime and reinforced brick work roofs.

He took courage to approach a big house and try his luck. The door was answered by a woman who seemed to be the lady of the house. Solomon knew that there would be no harm in trying and so he asked her for some food and told her the sad story of being "thrown out of home by his sister-in-law". As always, it worked like a charm. The lady, who was unrelenting at first, took pity on him and asked him to bring a banana leaf from the nearby garden. She then served him some food—rice and spicy curry of substantial quantity. Solomon had not had a full meal in many weeks. Months of staying on the streets had changed his habits. Instead of dawdling over his food as in old days, he would now finish it quickly after experiencing his food being snatched away. While Solomon was quickly scooping up handfuls of rice and curry, she enquired about his background, and advised him to go to the nearby town to look for a job.

Though he was happy about the food and the treatment he had received from the lady, in his heart he felt awkward and guilty about the whole thing. He almost cursed his fate which forced him to leave his home, the warm embraces of his family, and to stoop so low as to beg for food from someone else, that too by resorting to a cheap and petty lie. He slid into a pensive mood and reminisced about his grandfather's factory where many people were employed to earn enough to make a living. At his own home, poor people were fed. His mother had a habit of feeding at least two to five persons, mostly beggars, on every Friday noon. And today, he, the special son of that house, had to beg for food from someone! But what was preventing him from obeying the Master, who out of His mercy said, "Get up and go home"?

11

Converting Stumbling Blocks into Stepping Stones

Psychologists say that if one makes a decision at a momentous time using both one's brain and heart, one would stick with that decision, whether right or wrong. Scholars cite many examples from personal lives of people to substantiate this theory. More often than not, such decisions are taken impulsively without giving much thought to the consequences. Maybe that was true of Solomon, who decided in a weak moment to leave his home and ended up as a vagrant on the street. Though his behaviour seemed purposeless, it must have been God's plan to teach him about suffering, so as to later use him as an instrument to alleviate the pain and distress of other people.

After crying bitter and helpless tears the day before, Solomon started his next day in a morbid mood. He had no plan of his own but consciously submitted himself to the will of God. He decided to take each day as it unfolded. He proceeded to go to the next town and then eventually reach Madras, or Madurai, and try his luck at getting a job there. Gradually, his nomadic wanderings took him to Virudunagar.

The people in this town were deep-rooted in caste practices. The town had always faced an acute water shortage. It wore the look of an unorganized and unplanned town. It looks the same even today. Solomon decided he would try his luck and look for work at a hotel. He walked through the main road, looking for hotels. Though he had seen a number of small eating joints, he could not muster enough courage to step in any hotel and ask for a job. He continued to fidget with the idea of entering the hotels or not, and in the process, he not only lost more time, but also the little energy he had. As the skies turned a purplish blue and the descent of night was heralded, Solomon ended the struggle in his mind by entering into a hotel without thinking anything. He walked up to the hotel owner, and for the first time in three months, identified himself with his correct name and told him about his background. He mentioned the name of the district he belonged to, but withheld other details of his hometown or family, lest he should be transported there by the hotel owner. Although the owner was tough looking, hefty and huge, with a thick black moustache, he took pity on the boy and gave him some stale *idlis* and *vada* with *sambar*. Often those we think are incapable of love and affection are the ones who truly empathize with those who suffer and help them.

The hotel owner offered him a job as a table cleaner in his restaurant. He would be given three meals and tea and coffee in return. Further, if he worked well, he would be given a new dress within a week and, thereafter, new clothes every six months. Solomon was ecstatic beyond belief. It was the first time someone had trusted him and given him a full-time job. It sounded perfect—a new path was laid before him and his status had suddenly changed. He could finally bid goodbye to those days when he had to sleep on an empty stomach or try to quell his hunger pangs by drinking tap water from the railway station and lift heavy luggage from unfriendly and stingy passengers. Since he had not learnt the art of negotiation and bargaining, he readily agreed to all the conditions of employment. But for now, he pleaded that he be allowed to have a good sleep first so that he would be completely fit and rejuvenated the next day.

Solomon was asked to go upstairs to a makeshift thatched hall above the restaurant where about five others lived. There was also a small ill-maintained toilet-cum-bathroom open to the sky with makeshift walls. However, it seemed far more clean to Solomon who had had to make do with filthier public bathrooms and toilets. Solomon did not forget to thank God for giving him a safe place at last where he could lay his head down. It was a new beginning for him. He thought that if he continued in this job for some years, there was a possibility that he might establish a business firm, or a hotel, or even a service centre of his own, and then he could go back home proudly. He started dreaming about owning a big business establishment of his own or with other partners a few years hence. He was already pondering over the name of his new enterprise. "What should be the name if it happens to be a hotel?"; "What if it's a cloth mill?"; "Should I name it after my parents? Or may be any of my friends?"; "I could even use the name of a flower..."

With these jumbled yet happy thoughts, Solomon went into a deep slumber. The sun was already up and shining in his face brightly when he woke up the next day. He looked around and observed other workers going about their chores. Someone was engaged in cleaning the hotel premises, tables, and vessels, while the other was busy cutting vegetables and someone else was grinding rice or pulses. He saw a lot of hectic activity in the kitchen that was open to the sky so that the smoke from the wood fires would disperse easily. The master cook was in control of the kitchen with one or two assistants. Morning coffee was served to all. Since Solomon was new, the master directed him to clean the tables, to keep all the water glasses ready and also help in washing the plates and cups. He was given this assignment for a week. Once he successfully finished the 'apprenticeship period' in the cleaning department, he was promised the position of a server. Clearly, the hotel owner wanted to keep Solomon because he was the only one who was literate not only in Tamil, but also to some extent in English. The hotel owner himself was semi-literate.

The week passed quickly, leaving Solomon no time to think of the past days. He did a fairly good job, found favour with the owner, received new clothes and was promoted to the level of a table server. This was a very rare achievement by all means! He felt happy that within a matter of seven days he was promoted and also put on an impressive monthly salary of five rupees, apart from the food he had been promised. He was on cloud nine! This was a windfall for someone who had struggled so hard for a meal and had often starved. There was also the added luxury of being able to save some money.

Life's trials are ultimately what one makes of them. Though born in a middle class family, Solomon left home because of some money dealing with one of his friends in school. He was happy after a long time and he had found a new meaning in his life. The following Sunday, he decided to go to the local church for the first time in three months. No one in the church acknowledged his presence, or even attempted speak to him. If he had ventured to talk to anyone, no one would have come forward to interact with him. He was a stranger amongst them and they were wary of him. How far from the teachings of the *Bible* which directed the faithful to welcome strangers! But he was not bothered by this. He had gone to the church with the sole purpose of thanking God for bringing his life on the right track. Whatever he had in his pocket, he put it in the offertory. He returned to the hotel and shared his church experience with the owner. Though the owner was a Hindu, he was glad his employee was a religious person.

At times, he found the server's job to be too taxing. There were no fixed work hours and he ended up working 12 hours a day. Apart from that, the quality of the food offered was bad, and the servers had to face the brunt of criticism and abuses from the customers. Since in those days there were no refrigerators, the master cook always found novel ways of mixing the old leftover food with new dishes and gave them fancy names like *vadaikari* and *sambar vada*, which Solomon had to serve to the customers. He found the practice unethical and did not want to be a part of it, but there was no choice.

Hardly four weeks had passed by when Solomon felt the need to move to another town. Although to some extent, he liked the job as it gave him a roof over his head and food to eat, he was always under tension and stress that someone from his native place would come to the hotel. Solomon was scared that in case anyone discovered him, he would have to return home to face the consequences that made him break out in a sweat. He could not think that his parents would react differently. In his 13-year old mind, he had images of himself returning home having made it big. He did not want to be hauled back home like a truant kitten by the scruff of his neck, that too from a way-side hotel. What a come-down it would be! One morning, after getting a full month's salary, he left the hotel without telling anybody. He boarded a train from there and reached another town, Rajapalayam, on his way to Madras.

Solomon was now more confident that all the stumbling blocks in life could be converted to stepping stones. Working in the hotel for four weeks gave him the much-needed confidence to face any situation. It is strange that though many of us feel comfortable in our lives, sometimes we are under the influence of some force within us to face a situation or to quit. One could interpret that force to be divine or diabolic. No one knows why sometimes in life one walks away from the familiar to the unfamiliar and is catapulted to a new level of popularity and social recognition. Knowingly or unknowingly, sometimes one breaks new ground. Solomon too was now in a similar situation. Arriving in a new town and then wondering why he undertook the journey at all had now become a part of his everyday thought process.

Rajapalayam got its name from the name of the community that was dominant here—Rajas or Rajus of a Telugu-speaking community, who had migrated from

Andhra Pradesh centuries ago. The word *palayam* is frequently used in Tamil cities as a suffix and translates roughly to a 'fort'. Initially, Rajapalayam developed as an agricultural community. Due to the enterprising and hard-working nature of its people, commerce soon developed and several industries, particularly cotton-based industries, flourished. This gave the city the epithet of 'cotton city'.

In the 60s and 70s, handloom weavers conducted their weaving on the streets. This was for the first time that Solomon was witnessing weaving on such a scale. In his native place, there were a few families involved in handloom weaving, but this was a whole new experience.

It was fascinating for Solomon to see how the lengths of thread were straightened by stretching them over two wooden stakes driven in the ground. He saw the spindle flying across and the beautiful cloth emerging, iridescent like the feathers of a peacock. Down the street, there were some boys younger than he who were spreading a mixture of tamarind seeds onto the brightly coloured silk saris to stiffen them. As Solomon watched the various activities going on, he had no idea that a couple of decades later some self-styled champions on behalf of silkworms would threaten the livelihood of people such as these who were dependent on the silk industry. But then, those were different times and Solomon had not been exposed to questions where he would have to weigh the lives of silkworms against that of his fellow human beings.

Solomon tried hard but could not find any good job in this town. However, Rajapalayam had a considerably pleasant weather and this prompted him to stay on for a few days. He continued to look for a job. He was not keen on taking the job of a waiter in a hotel, though it had the thrill of entertaining people who came to eat. It also provided him with food security. But he feared that he would be spotted by someone from his family or his hometown. If someone noticed him, it would be impossible to give them the slip. On the other hand, if he were a porter, he could decide whom to approach and whom to avoid. People often choose to run away from their problems without realizing that one day problems are bound to catch up.

While he was roaming around from one street to another, his mind wandered to one incident that had happened almost two years ago. One day, while coming back from school with his friends, Solomon found a goat which he thought was stray. They started playing with the goat, gave it some leaves to munch on and made it follow them to their home. When they all reached Solomon's house with the goat following them, his mother asked them from where they found that goat. Each one started giving different answers to her. Solomon's mother was not convinced and she realized that it was not a stray goat but belonged to someone. She was also upset that her son was a part of that group who brought the poor animal so far away from its home only for their fun. She wanted to give him a sound beating but spared him because of the presence of other boys. She advised everyone, including Solomon, that one should have a heart 'of flesh and not of stone', and never to steal other's belongings and accept or receive anything from others without working for it.

With his mother's words ringing clearly in his ears, Solomon realized that begging or asking for something for free was against the principle his family stood for. He decided that he would never eat a meal he had not worked for. He also decided not to lie about himself to obtain favours from anybody anymore. He would heed what his mother had once taught him.

12

A New Benefactor

The next day when Solomon reached the bus stand, he spotted a group of daily construction workers waiting to be hired for the day. He was mistaken for a coolie by the head mason. He offered Solomon a job at the construction site as a helper to carry bricks and cement. Solomon jumped at the opportunity and grabbed the job. This was a whole new experience for him. He had never visited a construction site before, let alone work at one. Although his desperation had forced him to take up the job, it was a very difficult work. The work was continuous, starting at seven in the morning and lasted till about six in the evening. They were allowed a lunch break for about 30–45 minutes. But apart from that, there was no respite. Solomon had to carry planks with bricks and other material on his head. At the end of the hard day's labour, he got 50 paise. This was far less than the princely sum of five rupees he had got as a waiter but more than the money he used to earn as a porter. With that, one could easily buy one kilogram of fine rice and few vegetables in those days. In addition to that, all the construction workers were offered rice *kanjeee* (porridge) with black and green grams and some coconut during the midday. It was delicious and was high on nutrition. Though it was tough and required a lot of strength and energy, Solomon found this work better than looking for odd jobs at the bus stand. Besides, it earned him enough money with which he could buy breakfast and dinner. He could also afford bananas which he always relished and spare some money for ground nut candy.

Lifting heavy load and carrying tnem on his head on a daily basis gave Solomon a severe problem of cervical pain. Although the pain would vanish after a good night's rest, it would recur in the morning. At times, the neck would become very stiff, making it impossible for him to move or turn his head without turning his entire body. But with God's blessings, he was able to overcome this problem.

One day, when Solomon came to the railway station to sleep on his regular bench, he saw a man already seated on it, waiting to catch a train. Solomon maintained some distance and stood looking at him intently, waiting for him to leave 'his' bench so that he could rest his aching limbs. The man caught Solomon looking at him and found his expression rather curious. He suddenly had the urge to know the boy who was looking at him from a distance, quite evidently waiting for him to vacate the bench. So he called Solomon and enquired about his name and background. Solomon was quick to state that he was from Colachel, Kanyakumari District, and added that since he had no one to take care of him, he was working here as a labourer on construction sites. Solomon was greatly surprised at his reply. Quite unexpectedly, he had come out with half the truth about his life. In the course of the discussion, the man found that Solomon belonged to his own district, only about six kilometres from his place and that he went to the same school that he had gone to as a boy. He also learnt that Solomon had run away from his home because of some misunderstanding. He took pity on him and decided to help him.

For Solomon, the day ended with a taste of God's love expressed through the stranger. Clearly, there are people in the world who empathize with the poor and are committed to the cause of alleviating their suffering. These individuals have the love of God in them which urges them to do something for the needy. They do not anticipate worldly recognition for their simple acts of love. On the other hand, the so-called service organizations, even when they are involved in simple work, publish their acts of charity to earn popular recognition and acclaim along with material gains.

As the train was delayed, the gentleman spent more time with Solomon. The time the two spent together on the railway platform was not wasted. He tried to talk to Solomon and make him understand that he needed to get back to his native place and pursue his studies. He advised him to identify a relative who could support him. Solomon listened to him patiently but did not react. Although, he seemed like a nice man and whatever he was saying was for Solomon's benefit, the poor boy's exhausted body and tired mind did not allow him to react at all. All he was concerned with was to lie down on the bench and go off to sleep. However, the man, oblivious to Solomon's fatigue, went on and on, even listing examples of great leaders. He eventually decided to take the boy under his wings for a few days. Solomon, numb that he was with exhaustion, accepted and decided to go with him.

The gentleman's name was Radhakrishnan, an engineer by profession in the telephone department. He took Solomon to a nearby tent, 100 metres or so from the station where about 30 telephone workers stayed together and worked for the construction of telephone lines from one town to another. Mr Radhakrishnan was in charge of all these workers. He introduced Solomon to everyone and offered him a place of stay. Solomon was supposed to watch over the tent and other materials when the workers were away at work. In turn, he would be given food, new clothes and some pocket money. How the engineer developed such a genuine affection for him and also trusted him was a mystery to him. Was it because they both belonged to the same district and studied in the same school? Or was he a God-sent angel to help him?

With nothing to call his own and no support, Solomon had miraculously been elevated to a different level. He was now in charge of the valuables belonging to 30 workers and stock of various tools and accessories of telephones stored in the department. The copper wire used in the underground cables was costly and people stole them to sell them in the market. Besides the 30 workers, there was a cook, whom Solomon assisted in cooking. He used to clean the tent when the workers went to work and took care of all their belongings. When the workers returned in the evening, they would send him off on errands. Sometimes he was given small tips for these errands. Within a few days, all the inmates contributed some money and got him two sets of clothes. For the first time in his exile life, Solomon had a spare dress. At his home too, he was given new clothes on special occasions, like birthdays, festivals, school re-opening days and other ceremonies. He enjoyed his new life and the company of his new friends. Occasionally, he went to see movies with them. Being the only educated one from the lot, he wrote letters for them to their families. The irony of the situation was that though he helped others communicate their feelings to their loved ones, he had not thought of sending a letter to his own parents.

13

Reawakening of Faith

The next destination of the group was Madurai from where they had to lay down new telephone lines up to Melur. On the scheduled date, they moved out with bag and baggage to board a train to Madurai. For the first time in his exile life, Solomon was travelling with a valid railway ticket along with a group of people who cared for him. Till now, he was roaming around at the cost of the government. This time too he did not have to shell out money from his pockets as all was taken care of by the department. Solomon was very excited about his first 'legal' journey with a valid ticket. He did not need to worry about any burly policeman or any patrolling officer this time. No one would box his ears. After alighting from the train at the Madurai station, Solomon was exhilarated and completely charged up with energy. He was not unsure of this journey for he knew the purpose behind it. He was asked to carry the big vessel in which the cook used to prepare rice for everyone. Without any hesitation, Solomon carried the heavy vessel on his head and walked the entire stretch from the station to the place where they were supposed to set their base camp. He happily covered the entire stretch of three kilometres with the group, without feeling drowsy and droopy.

As he was walking joyously, he remembered the journey which he had taken with the rich old man and his helper at Sankaranairkoil. Though that journey was shorter than this, and also the load he was carrying then was lighter than the heavy-based vessel he was now carrying on his head, the load on his heart was way too lighter now. He felt as if it was divine grace that lightened the burden on his head and heart. The only difference between these two circumstances is that Solomon was now armed with greater vigour and a fresh outlook towards his life, and also because he was now accompanied by a group of people who cared for him. Solomon thanked God in his heart for His benevolence and for the mercy that He had showered upon him. Had God not helped him sail through rough waters, he would have long been swept away.

After walking a good distance of three kilometres, the team chose a good spot in Tamukkam ground to put up the tent for their stay. This ground dates back to the 16th Century, and was developed by Viswanatha Nayak, the first King of Nayak Dynasty in Madurai. When created, the ground was meant for sports and other events. Experts in different marital arts such as *silambu*, sword fight, etc., used to display their artistry at this ground. Similarly, sports events such as horse race, bull-fight, elephant race, etc., were also organized here. The place selected to set up the tent was much better than the previous one, for it was a good distance away from the station and was thus less noisy. Everyone in the group was delighted as there would be no clattering or raucous of hawkers or daily passengers. After spending the entire day at the site, all the workers came back to the tent where Solomon and the cook were ready to serve them food and help them by running errands for them. The team stayed there for about three weeks, completed the task well in time, and then moved about 15 kilometres further on the road to Melur and pitched their tent there.

While in Madurai, a town with rich history and many opportunities, Solomon made it a point to go to watch movies with his friends. At times, when the workers used to come back from the site at an early hour, they would all venture out in the city and enjoy a quick snack, or catch up the latest movie in the theatre. Solomon could not have asked for a better life! However, like everything good comes bearing the negative with it, Solomon's stay at Madurai had its share of grey streaks as well. Though they had camped at a place which was quiet and away from the din of the city, it was also an area secluded enough to be a favourite of pleasure seekers. Late in the evening, the area was used for immoral activities. Earlier on, Solomon never paid much attention to the various couples who came there, but soon got sceptical. Often men would come on bicycles or in cars and use the area to drink liquor and interact with women of loose morals. Though Solomon never really understood what happened at the place, nor did he bother to find out, he was sure that whatever was going on, it was surely unethical. Later still, he was shocked to learn that some his friends from the group too indulged in such activities. His friends, all of whom were much older than himself, would crack ribald jokes, often at his expense, which the boy would not understand. Some of them even went as far as to suggest that he too should indulge in those nefarious activities. This is not an uncommon situation, as reports have showed time and again that street children are often abused sexually, and more often than not, they are caught in the web of human trafficking and flesh trade. However, the boy was never abused by anyone in the group as some older men from the group had taken him under their wing; hence, Solomon was safe from the other dangers of street life. Otherwise, it was very easy to fall prey to vices on the street, which finally brings these street dwellers into conflict with the law.

One day while he was sitting in the tent, one of the senior engineers, who had passed through the area for his morning walk, stopped in front of the tent, and started questioning him about his background. Solomon did not know anything about the man, but later learnt that he was in charge of the entire district team. The man was wearing a simple dress as he was on his morning walk. Not wanting to waste his time on this conversation with a 'stranger', Solomon answered all his questions in a rather indifferent manner, almost to the extent of being rude. The engineer, though irritated, did not express his irritation forthwith. On returning home, he sent one of his men to bring Solomon to his home. The co-workers got a little worried about Solomon when they learnt that he had been summoned by their boss. They asked him to go to him politely. Solomon was understandably quite nervous, for he had never before been called by the senior.

When Solomon reached his house, the boss promptly informed him that he was the head of the team of workers and whatever job he assigned to the workers was to be done without any opposition. Solomon realized his folly and apologized for his behaviour in the morning. The engineer did not hold his grudge against the young boy for long and engaged him in light talk. Luckily for Solomon, he found favour in the eyes of the engineer. The engineer then proposed that Solomon could run some errands for him during the day, when he was not very busy at the tent.

In return, he would have a secure place to live in and good meals. Owing to his schooling, he was entrusted with tasks like running to the market to buy vegetables or other grocery. At times, he was even allowed to go to the market with the engineer's family in an old Fiat car. What a privilege! The food given to him, as promised, was finger-licking good. He relished it more so because it was non-vegetarian most of the time. After leaving his family, it was for the first time that he could eat non-vegetarian delicacies. He considered himself privileged to have a good place to stay in.

At times, the engineer gave him some pocket money as well. Never a day passed when he did not thank that engineer who had found him at the station platform and asked him to come with him and join the workers of the telephone department. That man, a junior engineer, was a Brahmin, whereas the family that took care of Solomon now were Muslims. This speaks volumes about the feeling of brotherhood among the people of India.

It was nothing but a quirk of fate and God's will which had prompted three people from different religions, cultures and caste backgrounds to come together. Evidently, they had mutual respect for each other's religion. They helped each other in times of need. It was strange for Solomon, having been born and brought up in a good Christian family and educated in a Christian school, now to live in the company of two others belonging to different cultural traditions. Except for him, there were no Christians in the entire group. It was but natural for a young mind like his to completely forget about going to the church, let alone reading the *Bible*. Not to place the blame entirely on him as he did not possess a *Bible*. However, it was unusual for a Christian boy not to possess one and neglect reading the *Bible* daily. It is true of all Christian families that *Bible* reading and prayers at home are taught as the cardinal principles to be faithfully followed everyday. Solomon too was brought up in that tradition. But his changed circumstances brought about the situation where he did not bother to own a *Bible*, or spend time in regular prayers.

While life sailed smoothly, one day the wife of the senior engineer asked him why, in spite of being a Christian, did he not go to church every Sunday. The question hit him hard and it came from unexpected quarters and at an unexpected time. It jolted him and pierced through him, shredding away the carefree attitude he had started to maintain towards his life and religion. He realized that as a Christian, he not only had the obligation of doing all things honestly, but also of going to the place of worship. It is said that a genuine Christian undergoes three conversions; first becoming committed to Christ, then to the church and then back to the world. Conversion is first of all an acceptance of Jesus Christ as one's personal Lord and Saviour. Once a person knows Jesus as the Saviour intimately, quite naturally he would want to be in fellowship with others who share the same faith. Fellowship with other believers is vital, entailing heavy responsibility to live in accordance with the Master's teachings by caring for the poor and the needy. A true Christian is expected to return to the world with compassion, love and care for others.

In everyone's life, at some point in time or the other, religion plays a crucial role. One may not proclaim his faith publicly or follow religious traditions and rituals, but he may spend time contemplating God and seeking His righteousness. The hours spent with the Almighty strengthen people and prepare them to face all adversities. Solomon knew all this too well, yet he had chosen to ignore it completely. He chided himself for the lack of gratitude he had shown towards God for his life and for helping him through the bad times. The woman's query about his indifference towards the church triggered a series of self-examining questions within Solomon, and much as he hated it, he felt ashamed of his selfishness. In his heart of hearts, Solomon knew that he had brought shame to his family in more than one way. Not only had he fled away from his home, resorted to certain unpardonable means to attain his bread and butter, he had even turned his back on his religion. The agony continued to bite him and he decided to put an end to all his adventures and return home.

Solomon thought about the story of the prodigal son mentioned in the *Bible*. According to the story, the son had forced his father to give him his share of the property and later wasted all his money in a far-away country. When he had nothing to eat and no means to acquire food, he went to the pigsty and sought to eat pods that the pigs ate. What a shame for the son of a big landlord, who had the means to feed a large number of people on his farm! It was then that the son thought about his father's wealth, care and love, and decided to go back home. His father, who was all the while waiting for his lost son's return, spotted him from a long distance, ran to him with an open heart, embraced him and took him home. He also arranged a big feast to celebrate the return of his prodigal son.

Standing in stark contrast to this story was another which Solomon had heard from his history teacher. A prince of a great king in India was severely punished for a grave mistake he had committed. The king had to allow his chariot to run over his own son to avenge the accidental killing of a small calf under the wheels of his son's chariot. Any of the two possibilities might hold true for Solomon also in case he returned home. His family would either welcome him back with open arms waiting to embrace him, or he would be punished so severely that he would never know the end of it! What was he to do? Solomon agonized over the 'should I or should I not' dilemma which had been ruling his life for quite some time now. Nevertheless, a tiny seed of hope was planted in his heart by that lady. It was up to him to nourish it with fresh positive reflection and prayer, or weed it out with poisonous thoughts of a carefree, egocentric pursuit of life.

Solomon felt very disturbed that night and the thought of returning to his parents continued to feed on his conscience. The thought of his parents, church, friends and others haunted him to such an extent that he could not even have his dinner. The very idea of eating food repulsed him completely. For the first time, he prayed to God very sincerely to keep everyone safe till he met them again. He was confident that all his tears and fears would disappear on the day when he would happily meet all his family members and friends. He had no idea of when that day would come. However, for some reason or the other, he could still not make the intended move. Each time he resolved to go back home, the possibility of the impending punishment always seemed heavier to him than the warm welcome the prodigal had received. He spent that night silently praying for God's guidance. How desperately he wished to possess a *Bible* then and there! Had he obtained a copy from somewhere, reading a few pages would have soothed him and helped him in his misery. The faith and trust, that one day he would meet all his family members and be with them forever, filled his heart, and with that, he closed his tearful eyes and went to sleep.

14

Moving Ahead

The following morning, Solomon woke up and got busy with his work as usual. Once again, the thought of going back home disappeared from his mind with the onset of work. But then he felt the strong desire to go to a church and seek a clear directive from God. After everyone left the tent for work, Solomon took the cook's permission and went out to look for a church in the town. After walking a great deal, he found one, much to his delight.

Solomon went in quietly and looked around with mesmerized eyes. The church, like all other churches, was not brightly lit. The altar was lit by numerous candles left there by the faithful, who had lit them in supplication or in gratitude for favours granted. The air smelt fragrant with the incense that had been burnt for the early morning service. The light from the candles cast flickering shadows on the paintings of the Virgin Mary and other saints. Looking up at the altar, Solomon felt that Christ's face was filled with sorrow at his foolishness. Solomon sank down to his knees at the nearest pew and gave himself up to the benevolence and grace of God as tears of contrition flowed down his cheeks. He prayed for forgiveness from the all-forgiving Father and for the safe-keeping of those whom he loved. After a while, when the storm of his emotions had abated, Solomon rose to his feet and dropped a coin in the offertory box. He wanted to feel the presence of God in the church, something he had often heard about, but he could not experience it. He was too innocent to understand it then that God bestowed his grace and love on all, and all he had to do was open his heart to Him. But young as he was, Solomon felt he needed to do something more. He resolved that he would one day go to Bethlehem, birth-place of Jesus Christ, and pray at the Church of Nativity, which is built over the humble stable where He was born.

He saw many people in the church. Some prayed with folded palms, some simply read the *Bible* silently and a few knelt and prayed at the altar with tears running down their cheeks. He also saw two or three boys, as old as himself, praying. He noticed a kind of calmness and peace on everyone's faces when they came out of the church. No wonder many go to different places of worship seeking peace for their souls. Personal stresses, adversities and pain lead people to find solace in spirituality. Those who had passed through a spiritual experience would say that they feel positive and enlightened. Solomon thanked the lady in his heart; had she not asked him about his lack of church visits, he would not have thought about church, prayer, worship and God's presence. She intervened to minister peace in his life, to reach out to God and seek solace for his drifting soul.

In the last four months, had others not loved him, sympathized with him, and looked after him at the bus stands and railway stations, Solomon would have been deprived of everything in life. Because of the love and care of these people, he could not only overcome deprivation, but also lead a fairly decent life. The one vital thing lacking was education. Even the senior engineer wanted to send him to school and directed him to get admission in a private school. But the school at Madurai refused to give admission to him without any details of his parentage, date of birth and previous school record.

It is here that we realize that the Maker of our lives has a plan of His own for each one of us, and He, at the appropriate time, acts and moulds us as per His plan. He is the potter who moulds clay into a vessel of his choice. Only at the right time will it serve the purpose for which it was created. As the *Old Testament* says, there is time for everything, a time to sow and a time to grow, a time for laughter and a time to weep, a time to let go and a time to keep.

After the Madurai-Melur telephone lines were laid, the workers wanted to take a short holiday before they embarked on a rather tough assignment at Munnar, where a new line was to be laid. Munnar is a hilly terrain and thus it is considered to be quite a difficult terrain to work on. All the workers were particular that they wanted to go home before this next assignment. The senior engineer offered to let Solomon stay with him while the others were away. Though he felt happy about the idea, somehow in his heart he was not at peace. Hence, he told him that he would also go home and come back to work with them at Munnar. Everyone in the group was astonished to hear him say this and were happy that he had chosen to return to his native place.

They mobilized money so that he could go home and even gave him some spare money if any contingencies at home were to arise. There were some in the group who suggested to him that he should now stay on with his family and pursue his studies if possible. They even offered to partly support him to meet the costs involved if need be.

A fantastic sponsorship idea thus came up from a group of workers who were yet to carve a life for themselves. They collected money from whatever little they earned and gave it to him. Solomon failed to understand what good deeds done by him were bearing such fruits that he had so many people who genuinely cared for him.

He was grateful for all the love and affection the workers had showered on him. As all were bidding him goodbye, there were some who encouraged him to come back because they wanted an educated boy and a trustworthy assistant in their routine work. They all asked him if he would ever come back, to which Solomon replied that he surely will, for he can never forget them all and what all they did for him.

None of them had any clue that once Solomon would reach home, his parents would never allow him to get back to this kind of a life, and they would educate him so that he can have a proper life—a life of possibilities, a life where there would be no place for regrets.

15

Having Cold Feet

The place where Solomon had spent many joyous days and nights with his group now bore a deserted look. Everything was packed up. The tent was dismantled and sent to the house of the senior engineer. Solomon, along with others, made his way to the bus stand. One of the elders, who happened to travel half way to his native place till Vallioor, volunteered to buy the ticket for him. Since there was no direct bus to his home town, Solomon got a ticket for the nearest town which was Nagercoil, the district head quarters. Though he himself had asked to be sent home, Solomon was beginning to feel the numbness creep up again. He was getting cold feet once more! While others talked animatedly about his return to his home, Solomon was seriously pondering over his decision. Should he go back home, or, as usual, choose another town for his living? He was still cogitating over this issue when the engine of the bus roared to life and the cranking of the gears informed him that he was now on his final journey; journey to his native home. Or so others thought!

The journey to Nagercoil took almost six hours. Another 23 kilometres by a local bus would take him to his hometown, where he expected to be before dusk. All the mathematics done, he still was not sure if he wanted to go back home!

As the bus rattled on, Solomon's mind jumped from one question to another. He wondered what reception awaited him. Would there be any display of hard feelings, or would it be an expression of pent up love and affection? Worst still, whether a stick awaited him! Love is the language every heart can understand and be comforted by. But if the language is one of hostility or abuse, what would he do? How would his friends react after his return? Would they treat him differently, calling him names and nagging him, or would they be too overjoyed to have their friend back? He knew that almost all his friends were now in the ninth standard, whereas he will have to be re-admitted to the eighth standard. His juniors, who knew him because of his splendid performances in campus activities, would now be sitting with him. Oh the shame! Would they welcome him with love and affection, forgetting the anguish he had caused them as their senior? Or would they shut the doors on him and turn hostile? His mind went back to his friend from whom he had borrowed Rs 25. That money was the reason he had to run away from his home. He had borrowed this princely sum for some extravagant expenditure, with the promise that he would return the money within a week's time. He had made matters worse for himself when he had proudly proclaimed that the other boy could complain to his parents if he failed to pay back the money. During the weekend, Solomon had tried everything he could to mobilize the amount, but he failed. Instead of staying put and facing the consequences of his actions, Solomon preferred leaving his home once and for all.

He was worried that his parents must have got wind of this money deal by now. Would they have repaid the sum? Would his friend have forgotten all about it? Or would his friend blame himself for being responsible for Solomon's disappearance? The crux of the matter was that he had run away from home because he was afraid of his moneylender friend.

After about four hours, the bus reached Vallioor. He now needed to travel only 35 kilometres in the same bus and then board another bus to reach Colachel. Solomon realized that he needed all his might to face his parents and others. If he obliged his weak heart, he would continue as a street boy, graduate into a rowdy, and who knows, he might even become a master criminal! Only God could infuse strength in him to gear up to face the situation when his self-confidence was at its lowest ebb.

Solomon resumed his calculations again. If he continued the journey, he would be home before dark. By then, his father would return from work. Since it was a Saturday, almost all his brothers would be home. There was a strict rule at home that the boys must return home by 6.30 pm on weekdays and by 7 pm on Sundays from the playground, or from the local library, or even if they had gone out with their friends to the beach.

The journey continued after a coffee break at a roadside hotel. Solomon quickly finished his snack. He was becoming tense with each passing moment. The thought of being branded as a bad boy by all, including his parents and his brothers, occupied his mind. Negative thoughts of not being accepted by the family raged within his heart. There was no one he could talk to as the older worker had got down at Vallioor. He broke into a cold sweat when the conductor called all the passengers to board the bus again.

Since Solomon was not at all in the positive-thinking frame of mind, his pessimism got the better of him. He asked himself, 'How can you ever dare to go back in this wretched condition?' The question horrified him. The thoughts about the punishment awaiting him turned his feet into lead. He felt terrible. He dragged himself towards the bus, still thinking about his decision and reprimanding himself for having spoken aloud about wanting to go back home in the first place. As other passengers were in a hurry to board the bus, lest they should miss it, Solomon was pushed inside in the melee and reached his seat without any effort on his part! To make matters worse, it was an express bus without any further stop *en route*, and before Solomon could even catch his breath to yell out to the conductor to stop the bus, the driver threw in the gears and started for the next stretch of journey to district headquarters Nagercoil.

16

Home Away From Home

After five months of mindless wandering, Solomon was bound for his home. Landscapes passed him by as he sat looking out of the bus window. No one had forced him to take this journey; he was himself responsible, for he had suggested to the engineer of the telephone department to permit him to leave for his home. Whatever had gotten into him! How could he push himself into this mess? Many jumbled thoughts were playing havoc in Solomon's mind. But one thing was certain—he could not go home like this. He decided that unless a miracle took place and he suddenly became rich and famous, he would not go back home. When he got off the bus at Nagercoil, he had completely turned his back on all thoughts of returning home. Instead of looking for another bus to take him to his native town, he turned towards the main town to look for work.

Solomon himself was not very sure as to what kept him from going home. He knew he had disgraced his family by running away, and worse still, by doing demeaning jobs as per the standards of his family. Like any child who did not understand the intricacies and complexities of human life too well, he was only concerned about whether or not he would be punished on returning home. He gave himself a self-explanatory speech that if he made it big, then no one would raise his hand against him. He thought that God must have something else in store for him and started looking around the town. He was so close to reaching home, yet he could not overcome the irrational fear in his mind and take that one step which would have taken him straight into the comforting fold of his family.

After idling away a week, Solomon started his hunt for job in Nagercoil. He thought that the best place to try out his luck would be the market area. On arriving there, Solomon looked around a number of shops and spotted a sweet shop. He went in and approached the owner of the shop, who was a Muslim. He was a well-known person in the area and people addressed him as *Bhai* (elder brother). When Solomon asked him for a job, he looked the boy over and looked at his face. He not only offered him a job—

which was to clean pulses and millets—but also offered him a place to stay in his home. He had four children—two by his first wife, who had died few years ago, and two by his second. During his stay at the shop owner's house, Solomon was never made to feel that he was only a servant at the shop. *Bhai* advised him to live upstairs along with his first wife's children and eat his meals at his home like one of his children. It was indeed a privilege bestowed upon Solomon by the Almighty. Till about four months, Solomon had to live on the streets without any provisions, let alone a proper house and meal. Then God's blessings were showered upon him in the form of the group of workers with whom he lived in a tent with adequate care. But none of these experiences provided him with the love and care of a family, something which Solomon missed the most during his exile. It was now that the void had filled as *Bhai* and his wife always treated him as one of their sons and cared for him.

Solomon's day started at seven in the morning, when he used to accompany *Bhai*'s elder son and open the shop. Thereafter, he was kept relatively busy in cleaning the shop, preparing the pulses, ground nuts, and other material required for the preparation of sweets. The entire day's preparations were then sold. The cash counter was administered by *Bhai* and in his absence by his elder son.

Initially, life at the shop was very difficult for Solomon. He had almost no experience in separating the dirt from the pulses and that too in large quantities. Back home, his brother was the one who used to help his mother in the kitchen. Solomon too had helped his mother at times in whatever possible manner he could. He had helped her in separating the stones from rice. But then the rice was in small quantities. Here the task was 100 times more. The hearth at the shop was also quite big and required continuous firewood to keep it hot enough through out the day. Solomon was involved in all these activities. He had to carry firewood from the backyard of the shop to the main kitchen area. Till noon, his life seemed completely torturous to him as he never had to put in so much of work ever.

It was only in the afternoon that he used to get some respite from the laborious tasks that he was supposed to do. He made use of his free time by visiting the temple tank in the town to have a bath and eat his lunch. Apart from that, he never ventured out for any kind of sightseeing or fun activities. He stayed at the shop to respond to any call from *Bhai,* if in case he needed his assistance. The work Solomon did in today's parlance was nothing but child labour. But then he had no choice, he had to work to earn his livelihood. There was no other option open to him.

Everyone in the family was fond of Solomon. He had earned the entire family's love and affection by showing his dedication towards his work. He was treated like an equal by them. Never did the thought that he was, after all, a servant in their shop cross the mind of anyone in the family. Initially, they were a bit wary of him. They were a little apprehensive that he might be a runaway and soon his family members will come looking for him. They accepted his story of being an orphan with some reservation. But the sincere hard work that he put in his work day in and out won them over. For them, he was beneficial in many ways as he was an educated boy. Slowly, he gained their confidence and was put in charge of the cash counter. Solomon always remained truthful to his work and never betrayed the trust reposed in him.

There was a time in Trivandrum, where he had stayed for a few weeks, when he could hardly earn 25 paise a day. But now he handled the affairs of a sweet shop that did relatively good business and handled money in various denominations. He had once transacted a hundred rupee note also. *Bhai* often said, "Whenever Solomon sits in the *kalla* (the cash counter), the sales are very brisk." It was always a proud moment for Solomon whenever he was appreciated thus. He was riding a high wave of luck and blessing. His good reputation allowed him to avail of leisure time for himself when he could go out for some entertainment or watch a movie. He could even use *Bhai*'s name in nearby hotels and shops to buy whatever he wanted. This was truly a privilege. For Solomon, it was a blessing from God. He felt intuitively that later on in his life God would bless him with more and more money. He also prayed for such a status in life. He assumed that this was an indication of what was to come in his life. He could foresee a blessed life for him with abundant wealth. He started daydreaming of a bright future. His mind was like a pendulum, swinging from one end to the other, sometimes thinking negatively and lying low in spirit, and at other times, thinking positively with his spirit soaring. When his spirit dipped low, he always imagined himself leading life as a poor fellow on the street pulling carts!

17

Bitter Taste of Humiliation

It was in Nagercoil that Solomon found the love and care of the family, and it was here that he had to partake of the bitter taste of casteism for the first time. Caste system is one of the evils that still continue to eat into the foundation of India, perpetuating and feeding illiteracy, deprivation and poverty. However, recent research indicates that before the arrival of the British, though the caste system existed, there was not much discrimination of one community against other, and disparities in economic status were not as glaring as they now are. Research attributes the present socio-economic differences among the communities to the British rule and the adoption of the hierarchical system by the Indian rulers. Governance based on hierarchy of social status or positions of authority only strengthened the caste system in the country. It is nothing but a misinterpretation of the classical Vedic system. Nevertheless, the caste issue is a setback for the progress of India and strikes at the root of spiritualism.

Until now, Solomon had not encountered any kind of discrimination. He belonged to the Nadar Christian community, a community that has held the pride of being educated even before India gained its independence. In fact, until the 60s and 70s, people from this community held high positions in government departments and teaching jobs. However, this profile altered gradually around the mid-1960s. Apart from the stronghold of 45 per cent Nadars—both Hindus and Christians—there were other communities as well, including 20 per cent fisher folk, 15 per cent Muslims, 10 per cent Nairs of Kerala, and other Backward and Schedule Castes constituting 10 per cent of the total population. Solomon never faced the issue of casteism despite living in such a diverse society. He had friends and classmates from all the communities.

As part of his job at the sweet shop, Solomon had to fetch water each morning from different public taps from the streets in a bucket for cleaning the shop. Thereafter, he sprinkled water in front of the shop. One day, Solomon went to the nearby street tap to fetch water as usual. In the 60s, water was supplied to families either directly through a separate pipe or groups of families were allowed to draw water from a common public tap. That day when Solomon went to fetch water, he saw a *kudam* (a vessel made of copper with a narrow neck and a wide mouth) filled with water. Solomon thought that someone must have kept the *kudam* underneath the tap but could not return in time to take it or close the tap. So he decided to set it aside and then placed his *valli* (a big bucket) there. Suddenly a lady approached him and asked him how dare he touch her *kudam*! She scolded him pitilessly and abused him in front of everyone present there. Later, she poured away the water on the ground and then cleaned the vessel with red mud and once again filled it with water from the tap.

Solomon did not understand the meaning of all this but felt extremely embarrassed since the woman had abused him in front of others. When she was shouting at the top her lungs at him, he had looked uncomfortably at others around him. Some looked at him with pity, few expressed anger at him, and yet, there were others who supported his behaviour. Solomon could not fathom any reason for being treated thus. Was he not correct when he thought it best under the circumstances to remove the vessel rather than wasting precious water? With a glum look on his face, he went back to the shop and narrated the incident to *Bhai*. He understood what would have been the problem and told Solomon that he should have gone to one of the Konars' streets to fetch water. After receiving a quizzical look from

Solomon, he explained to him that since Solomon was dark-complexioned, the lady must have thought that he was an untouchable and so admonished him with such abusive language. It was for the first time that Solomon had first-hand experience of the ever-prevalent caste system in India. He not only felt bad because the woman had behaved so badly, but also felt the plight of the so-called lower caste families in the villages. He was reminded of one of the lessons of Mahatma Gandhi which he read in school. "God never made man so that he may consider another man an untouchable!" His mind also went back to a passage he had read in the *Bible*: "There is neither Jew nor Greek, slave nor free male nor female; for you are all one in Christ Jesus." It is difficult to see how in God's eyes, differences could exist between different religions, castes and races. While in school, he had never grasped the full meaning of the verse of St Paul. He now understood the true meaning and imbibed it in his heart. It is not the colour or creed of an individual or community that matters in the world, but the way one conducts oneself in public and becomes an instrument for the betterment of other people's lives that matters.

This incident left a big scar in his mind. Prior to this experience, he had no idea that there existed different castes in Tamil Nadu, of which a few are considered forward, the majority as backward and a sizeable population is considered as scheduled caste and scheduled tribe. These differences are not as prominently displayed in big towns and cities as in remote areas. In rural areas, there are still a few pockets where caste discrimination is evident during temple festivals and in the fixing of marriage alliances.

Solomon later learnt from others that his community was classified as a backward class in the official list of castes. A majority of the population in the country is classified as being backward, whereas the so-called forward and scheduled castes are 3 per cent and 20 per cent respectively. That day, when he was so badly humiliated because of the woman's perception of his caste, he decided never to discriminate against others or mistreat others on the basis of their caste, creed or religion. Moreover, he vowed that in future, if given a chance, he would work more and more for the economically backward and uplift all marginalized groups, including those who were discriminated against on the basis of their caste. Economic empowerment is an effective weapon against ancient caste prejudices. As people progress to higher economic status, caste-based biases will surely fade away. The owner of the sweet shop understood that the incident had affected the boy and granted him a brief respite in the evening and directed him to spend an hour every day in the local library. 'Spend the time reading' is the most valuable advice that can ever be given to the youth.

As directed by *Bhai*, Solomon started going to the local library. In his hometown, he used to go to the municipal reading room along with his friends. Back then, he used to read comic books or the local vernacular language papers.

Once the owner told him to visit the reading room, he thought that this was the best place to rekindle his spirit to read small stories.

The library study hours, which were an after-effect of the incident which left Solomon badly affected, proved to be a blessing in disguise for Solomon. Once he began reading the daily papers, the first thing he saw each day was the advertisements put by parents and relatives of missing children. He knew immediately that his parents would have placed similar announcement in the papers. He felt disappointed for not having read any newspaper in the past five months. The thought that they might not have advertised at all too occupied his mind. But still he asked the men in the reading room to supply him with old newspapers so that he could check. No one was of much help in the matter. Solomon thought that he was the most unfortunate fellow in the world as he missed the possibility of his parents locating him. Only a few weeks back, he had got down from the bus that was to take him to his home, and now here he was repenting his lack of reading newspapers which snatched away the possibility of his parents locating him! The first week that he spent in the library looking for the advertisement placed by his parents was agonising for him. He hardly read any news or stories. However, he made it a regular habit to visit the library.

One day during one of his leisure times, Solomon noticed lorries bearing the name of Ramalingam & Co, plying between his native town Colachel and other places transporting Palmyra fibre. As soon as he read the name, he felt that it was somehow familiar, but he was not very sure where had he read it before. He went about his work the entire day but his mind was preoccupied with the name of the company. Just as he was about to sleep, it dawned on him that it was the company that his father worked for. A chill went through his spine. He felt his stomach collapse in a knot. There was an unexplainable anticipation and excitement in his body as soon as he learnt that the lorries of that company ferry to and fro Colachel. Suddenly, a novel idea struck him. He could use the lorry service as a communication link with his parents. He thought that there was a chance the lorry drivers and cleaners would meet his father. Solomon tried to find out more about the lorries and learnt that the lorry drivers stopped at the same restaurant where he occasionally went in for a snack. He started writing letters and flagged them on the ropes which were used to bundle the bales of Palmyra fibre. He was sure that the cleaners or the load men would see the letters while untying the ropes, and then they would pass them on to his father. Solomon was a sure believer in miracles. He thought about the joy his family would feel on receiving the letter from their son. 'Oh! They would be so delighted to learn that I am alright,' he thought. The poor lad did not think for once that his letters might fly away in the wind, thanks to the speed with which the lorries travelled.

Solomon waited endlessly. Each day the lorry came back to Nagercoil and he would purposely stand in front of the people descending from the lorry, lest one of them recognized him and handed him a letter from his parents. But that day never came. Frustration was now marked each time on his face as the lorry was emptied and no one even passed a look at his side, let alone hand him a letter. Miserably disappointed, Solomon thought that his family had forgotten him. He did feel bad that his parents never bothered to reply back, but then reminded himself that he need not worry about it since he had never, in any of his letters, mentioned about his whereabouts. He comforted himself with this and also felt that he need not worry about anything now or even repent running away from home, for Bhai's family was taking care of him.

18

The Prodigal Returns

Solomon was thankful that he had the support of a good, loving and caring family. He realized that material success might give just physical solace, whereas the care and love people showed to one another would bring ever-lasting peace and joy. Things were shaping up pretty nicely to the best advantage of this school dropout because of the magnanimity and mercy of others. However, he soon realized that money and security may not be the solution for all his problems. One needs to do something more to achieve contentment. What is it that each one of us is expected to do and how we should get involved can only be directed by

God. He only moulds us to act rightly so that our calling becomes effective and meaningful in totality.

At times while in bed or while in the reading room, and sometimes even when working in the shop, Solomon wondered what his calling was and how long he would continue like this. Would there be an end to his physical struggle? He always thought about what his Sunday school teacher Miss Baby Florence, who also happened to be his aunt, said. According to her, everyone had a calling from God. 'What is my calling?' He started wondering about his life and the call.

Was it his call to live away from his kith and kin and be with another middle class family belonging to a different religion, supporting them to do their business? Was he supposed to be a labourer in someone's family? Was he a vessel created by God in order to glorify His name? Day after day, Solomon pretended that he was happy, but deep inside he felt a vacuum that made his life evidently purposeless. There was an emptiness in whatever he did. There was a craving to go home, but then something held him back. He wanted to be happy, but much that he tried, he failed miserably. He wanted to see his parents again, wrap his arms around the warm comfort of his mother, eat delicious food cooked by her, and hear her singing devotional songs. He missed the pillow fights with his brothers without which none of them went to sleep. He longed to see his friends and crack jokes with them on books, other friends and strangers.

He wanted to play with his fellow students. He wanted to walk on the road in his town where most of the passers-by recognized him.

He knew that excepting God, no human being on earth could discern his life's purpose and that all his so-called happiness and confidence were only petty masks meant to cover up the vacuum which had formed a stronghold deep down in his heart. The agony and anguish of being away from home had affected him greatly. It was not easy for him to accept the fact that he yearned for his home, family and friends, though he tried to run away from them. 'What is my calling?' he repeated the question to himself. Did God really have a plan for his life? Or was this all that was there to it? He again started depending on God to guide him further.

One day when he came out from the library, he noticed a group of men at the bus stand. Something made him feel that they were related to him. But since he was not very sure, he decided to go close, but not close enough, and observe them. From their conversation, he learnt that they indeed were distant relatives of his father. He figured that they had come to this town to attend a wedding. Immediately, his thoughts jumped to his parents. Were they also here? The mere thought froze him to his soles. Though for the past few days he was badly missing his family and he knew that he would be completely overwhelmed to see them, but he was also not very sure if he really was ready to go back to them. What would happen if they spot him? All hell will break loose for sure. In his unconscious ingenuousness, he played with the idea that if at all his parents spotted him here in the market, he would go down on his knees and ask for their forgiveness for his silly behaviour. In his anxiety, Solomon had even prepared the pardon speech that he would say before them. But then, suddenly his thoughts went back to his new 'foster' parents. He did not want to leave them abruptly and join his family. The thought wrecked him. Since he could not foresee as to what would happen to him if he returned back, he thought it was better if he did not take the chance in the first place.

While Solomon was exploring options for his escape, one man in the group noticed him. He drew everyone's attention towards Solomon, and began walking towards his direction. As soon as Solomon saw them approaching him, he apprehended trouble. God surely did not wish to favour him any more, he thought. For a split second, he was almost paralysed with fear. The entire scene had taken a flip. For better or for worse, that was left to witness. Without thinking anything, Solomon rushed towards his master's shop. The group, his relatives, also followed him to the shop. Solomon chided himself for going to the market. 'Why could I not stay at the shop?,' he thought miserably. When he saw them approaching the shop, he ran to the owner's house. He did not say anything to anyone at the shop. He could have swiftly reached the bus stand and left the town, but he did not do so. He only wanted to go to *Bhai*'s house to ward off the impending trouble from himself. On reaching the shop, the group started making enquiries from the people there.

Many a time, what we think might be the best solution may not turn out to be as good. Had Solomon ran off to some other direction, his relatives would not have gone to the shop where he worked. Things were now closing in on him. The visitors were in front of the shop asking for him. *Bhai* stood there looking surprised at whatever the visitors had to say or ask about Solomon. He informed them that a boy named Solomon had been working at his shop for the past two months. From the answers they received, the relatives were fully convinced that the boy who ran away after seeing them was indeed the 'lost prodigal son' of Raj, their relative.

When *Bhai* informed them that the boy who had been working for him was an orphan, it sounded like a bitter and harsh word to the visitors. He also told them that he was very good in his work and added that he treated the poor kid like his own son. For a moment, the relatives thought that it was a case of mistaken identity. But since they were doubtful, they gave *Bhai* all the details about Solomon. He was greatly surprised to learn that Solomon was not an orphan but the son of a respected family. In the meantime, neighbours from other shops had also gathered in front of *Bhai*'s shop. Initially, everyone was under the impression that Solomon had caused come trouble to the visitors. But on being told about the background of the boy, they also joined in with *Bhai* and vowed that Solomon was a good boy.

Once everything was clear, a greatly surprised *Bhai* proudly announced to everybody that the boy working for him was not an orphan but came from a respected middle class family. He was proud of the fact that he had given shelter to a boy from a good family for two months. The visitors realized that had it not been for *Bhai*, Solomon would have become a vagabond. They thanked him for all that he had done for the boy and wanted to take him immediately under their custody. But better sense prevailed on *Bhai* and he told everyone to be calm and be happy about the turn of events. He said that taking Solomon immediately would upset him, and thus asked the visitors to return to their town. He promised them that he would restore the child to his parents.

Solomon had no idea as to what had happened in the shop after he had left. As usual, he had dinner with the family and went to bed. *Bhai* came very late and behaved normally in front of Solomon, as if nothing had happened. When they all went to sleep, Solomon tossed and turned on his bed. Sleep completely eluded him. He was feeling uncomfortable with what had happened. He was sure that since his relatives have seen him in this town, they would inform his parents, who would come looking for him. Moreover, he could hear *Bhai* saying something to his wife in a hushed voice. He could hear him voicing his concern and confusion. From what he managed to catch, *Bhai* was expressing his doubts about the boy, thinking that he had been lying to them for so long. He did not understand what had prompted Solomon to hide the real facts about himself from the family. *Bhai* was also sceptical if it was all a gimmick played by the locals to get the boy out of the shop and get him to work for them. Solomon suspected something was wrong but felt happy and contended that he was still in his adopted home.

The next day when *Bhai*'s elder son and Solomon were about to leave for the shop, *Bhai*'s wife informed them that the shop was closed on account of a local festival. She asked them to stay home. After some time, *Bhai* got ready and gave the boys new clothes. They were very happy as they anticipated that they would get a chance to see the local festival. They were even more delighted when they saw a taxi outside the house. This was a rare privilege and they looked forward to enjoying a splendid day.

As he was about to get in the taxi, *Bhai*'s wife called Solomon and gave him a small parcel and pressed a few notes into his hands without anyone noticing the gesture. She looked at his face dearly and said, "Goodbye Solomon. Take care of yourself." Solomon instantly sensed sadness in her face and voice. He asked Mohammad, the elder son, whether she was upset that she was not part of the group that was headed for the celebrations of the local festival. Since Mohammad knew the main purpose behind this journey, he stayed mum. Solomon, on the other hand, thought that she had given him the money so that he could spend it at the festival with Mohammad. 'What a caring lady', he thought. He did not realize that it would be the last time he would ever see her. For the past eight weeks, when he was with the family, she looked after him like her child. She had never discriminated between her children and Solomon.

After a few miles of travel, Solomon sensed that something was wrong about their journey. It slowly dawned on him that it was "mission of reunion" and he was headed towards his home. He was escorted to his home by *Bhai*, his son Mohammad and *Bhai*'s friends. Deep down in his heart, he felt very uncomfortable. He was devastated. What could he do now? He felt like pushing himself out of the car. He could only think of the severe thrashing he will receive by his parents in front of these people. Tears streamed down his cheeks. Mohammad tried to provide him some kind of consolation and assured him that nothing would happen to him when he reached his home and that everything would be for the better. Though these were words of comfort, Mohammad himself was very upset as he would be losing a dear friend. As his hometown came nearer, Solomon felt ashamed for what he had done, for all the hurt and pain he had caused to his family. He was afraid that his father, mother and brothers would not speak to him and would close the door on his face. After a long drive, except for a brief stop for lunch at one of *Bhai*'s friends' place, the taxi reached Colachel.

It was around six in the evening when Solomon landed at his home. Everyone had been eagerly waiting for his arrival. There was a huge cry of ecstasy among the members of the family at the historic reunion. Solomon's mother, as soon as she saw her son, came running towards him, embraced him and kissed his forehead repeatedly. Solomon only had tears in his eyes and could not even utter a single word; he could not even muster enough courage to apologize for his behaviour. In her touch, he could feel the warmth which assured him a new life of security, care and love.

Solomon's father, normally a quiet and reticent gentleman, could not hide his tears that day. He held his son and told him not to cry any more. His body language and facial expressions conveyed to Solomon that he wanted to say that enough is enough and now it was time to forget the past. His father's grip on his body gave Solomon the much-needed strength.

All his brothers looked on with tears streaming down their faces. They maintained a calm atmosphere and let the parents rejoice the return of their son. They were only waiting for the time when they will be able to talk to their brother alone. Neighbours had also joined in the reunion procession. Solomon, despite of all the new found love and affection, was not feeling comfortable. He could not say anything other than "*Amma*" and "*Pappa*". He could ask for forgiveness from his father like the prodigal son in the *Bible*. But he just stood there saying nothing. However, the tears in his eyes told his parents everything they wanted to know or hear.

In the meantime, Solomon's father had ordered dinner for everyone from a nearby hotel and everyone had supper together. *Bhai* and his son were thanked profusely by Solomon's father and other relatives who had come to welcome Solomon back. Solomon's father held *Bhai*'s hand, while the latter narrated how the boy had come to him and the day his relatives had spotted him in the market. Solomon shamefacedly apologized to *Bhai* for having lied to him that he was an orphan. *Bhai* told him that he was fortunate to have a family and never to say that he was an orphan. After dinner, *Bhai* and his son prepared to return back. Solomon's mother came with a packet which she said was for *Bhai*'s wife and thanked them both in a voice chocked with emotion for having taken care of her son and bringing him back. They took leave of Solomon's family and walked back to the taxi with mixed feelings. During the past two months, they had grown very fond of Solomon. But they also knew that it would have been wrong to keep him away from his family just because of their attachment with him. Although there were assurances from both sides to keep in touch, they all knew that it was not possible to do so as their worlds were so different.

As the taxi finally sped away in a cloud of dust, Solomon suddenly felt very tired after all the excitement of the day. All he wished for was that night would soon fall. He longed to lie on the bed, indulge in a deep slumber and try to forget all that had happened in the day. He was now finally at peace. His family was there to provide him with mental, emotional, spiritual and physical support so that he could face the world more confidently. This was God's love manifested through others. Solomon, the prodigal, who chose life on the streets, was now brought back to where he belonged. He felt both embarrassed and happy.

Why he had to traverse this path, no one could figure out. He had experienced poverty, deprivation, discrimination, untouchability, despair, love, care, and support. He had been penniless, without the basic necessities of life. He had to lie about his family, had to fend for himself, sleep on benches, on the bare floor in railway stations, and on the street during summer and rainy days without any roof over his head. In a sense, he was moulded to be a different boy. Why did he run away from home on account of a silly reason? It was a question his parents, brothers, and friends, asked him over a period of time. All of them wondered whether the Lord had a purpose in making the boy endure all these travails. Was He showing him the sufferings of the poor so that he would work tirelessly for the weaker sections later in life? No one knew but that could be the truth. At this point, all that they did was to celebrate the homecoming of the prodigal boy.

His father put an end to all the questions that were being asked of the boy and declared that everyone was to forget the episode and treat it like a bad dream, if not an experience of the world. The boy was not to be bothered about his past life any more. His father encouraged his son to face his future with confidence. "Let us instill courage in him to face the present with confidence and the future with expectancy," he said. The boy felt there was no place like home.

Solomon's mother, having heard her son's account, once again recollected the dream she had in 1946, at the time of his birth, and advised him to build a church in later years of his life. Late at night, when he was in bed, Solomon only hoped and prayed that one day he would help the vulnerable. The story of Solomon stands out as a miracle, whereby God Almighty had guided him through various realities of life and probably wanted him to be His agent of change in service to others. That must have been His purpose for his exile. If so, the greatest challenge to him would be to translate God's wishes into reality. Did he live up to the call? To a great extent, yes. In later years, Solomon worked in the development sector in various capacities and brought new hope and light to many families. Although he is now in his 60s, he still serves as a guide, friend, mentor to many, and works as the chief executive officer of a large development organization and continues to be an instrument of change in the lives of the vulnerable. How he made it is another story, if not a witness to write!

About the Author

Sixty-three years old R Bhakther Solomon is the CEO of an NGO working for developmental works in South India. He is a post graduate in Economics from the Madras University. Search for knowledge took him to various short duration courses within India and abroad. This included a specialized short training programme from the prestigious Indian Institute of Management, Ahmedabad; Reading University, UK; INODEP, Paris; Scale-up Institute, New Hamphire College; Graduate School, Manchester (USA); and Credit Union Foundation, Australia. He is widely travelled and has visited more than 25 countries.

As a social scientist studying human behaviour, the author has keenly studied children and their predicaments. As a child, he suffered the fate of Solomon, the hero of this book. The book is actually his story that kept him hooked to the lasting memory of his childhood. He has achieved a rare blend of autobiographical realities with child psychology. No wonder that the hero Solomon bears the same name as his.